The NATURE of Investing

The NATURE of Investing

Resilient Investment Strategies through Biomimicry

KATHERINE COLLINS

First published by Bibliomotion, Inc.
39 Harvard Street
Brookline, MA 02445
Tel: 617-934-2427
www.bibliomotion.com

Printed in the United States of America

CIP data applied for

To my parents, who have taught me
honor and service and faith and love.

To my siblings, who have taught me
kindness and generosity and devotion.

To our next generations.

And to yours.

Contents

Part I: Preparing the Ground

Saved By the Bee 3
The Roots of Biomimicry Investing 13
The Roots of Biomimicry Practice 19

Part II: Re-Rooting Investing: Six Transformations

From Efficient to Effective 27
From Synthetic to Simple 49
From Maximized to Optimized 71
From Disconnected to Reconnected 95
From Mechanical to Mindful 117
From Static to Dynamic 137

Part III: Cultivation and Care

Biomimicry Investing:
Resilient, Regenerative, Reconnected 159
Timshel: The Power of Choice 165

Notes 169
Resources 181
References 187
Acknowledgments 197
Index 201
About the Author 209

When we try to pick out anything by itself, we find it hitched to everything else in the universe.

—John Muir

There can never be good for the bee which is bad for the hive.

—Ralph Waldo Emerson

PART I

Preparing the Ground

Saved by the Bee

One of my most treasured possessions is the gift my father gave to me when I started my first job: it's a sign from IBM, circa 1970. My dad worked there for many years, and so our entire family was constantly surrounded by this motto. Every pencil, every notepad, every coffee mug held this simple command, in classic typewriter font:

`THINK.`

This sign has come with me everywhere, from a little cubicle with a scenic view of the ventilation shaft to a big corner office, and it's only recently that I realize what a true gift it was: embedding in my mind, from my earliest memory, the idea that when you go to work, your job is to THINK.

For more than twenty years I've been a professional investor, and this is what I love most about my profession: it requires you to think, in a proactive, engaged, creative way. Partly that's due to the fact that the world is always changing. Of course, things have been shifting within the investment business too. In fact, it's hard to overstate the changes in the structure of our financial markets just over the last twenty years or so.

Take one small example of an investment tool: the heat map. Twenty years ago, heat maps—those red and green patchwork charts that display stock prices on every TV finance channel and every investing website—did not exist. In fact, when I started as an investor, the Quotron was still our main source of stock prices, and it was down the hall, shared by about a dozen people. This was not an elegant piece of technology: the Quotron weighed at least fifteen pounds, it required a dedicated phone line, and it had one of those tiny green screens that quivered with the sheer physical effort of transporting small bits of data. You had to manually enter each ticker symbol, which led to some long lines around the machine, especially on days when a lot was happening in the stock market.

But the Quotron, precisely because it was so user-unfriendly, brought a great advantage. It was our water cooler. If you were a semiconductor analyst, this is where you learned about oil prices. If you were a retail analyst, this is where you learned about housing starts. You knew which industries were doing well just by the look on your colleagues' faces as they checked their top holdings. That crowd around the Quotron connected our individual pods of data into a web that was more like knowledge, and sometimes even wisdom. Just as importantly, it connected us to one another.

There is no question that the heat map is a better, easier tool to use for data on stock prices. And these days, you don't need to be a professional investor to access all of that data every second of every day, right from your cell phone. But something has been lost amidst this efficiency: those hallway conversations have disappeared. The perspective, the exchange, the connection provided in that water cooler setting—that's not something I can carry in my pocket. It's still out there, but it's farther away than ever.

This cycle of technological improvement has repeated itself over and over again, with most of our new tools and products and processes bringing big gains in efficiency or speed or scale. But gradually, many of these advances have chipped away at the connection—connection to the world, and to each other—that has always been at the heart of the investment profession.

As the investment business was evolving in this direction over the years, I felt more and more a sense of personal struggle. I couldn't quite define its source, or even recognize the strain, but at one point during my last few years of money management, I had a long day of client meetings, about a dozen in a row. At the end of the day I realized that every single client had asked me questions about portfolio statistics like tracking error, but only one client had asked anything about an actual investment I'd made—what the company did that was of use to the world, what made it worthy as a place to deploy our shareholders' funds.

Soon after this, in the face of a tiny market correction in 2006 (nothing like what we were to see a couple of years later), my funds underperformed by ten times more than any of our fancy risk-management models said was possible. Over the course of the next year, my funds recovered and outperformed again, but even after this small crisis passed, I felt a deep sense of dis-ease. I feared that my profession was evolving in a direction that was foreign to me. I feared that the tools we'd invented to help us invest wisely were beginning to pull us off course. Importantly, this was not a question of wanting a new job, or even a new career. Investing is my *vocation*—and the idea of splitting from one's vocation, well, it's just heartbreaking.

Fortunately, in the midst of all this struggle, I found the honeybee.

More precisely, I found Dr. Tom Seeley, the noted honeybee researcher from Cornell University. Dr. Seeley's recent work has been focused on collective decision making within beehives. It turns out that bees are not just pretty good at decision making, or above average. They are fantastic! For example, bees choose the best available hive location almost every time when they are getting ready to swarm to a new home.

Dr. Seeley's work is amazing from a scientific standpoint, but what really struck me was the conclusion of his talk, when he described the key characteristics that enabled the bees' optimal decision making.

- **First, bees go out into the world to gather data.** When they have an important decision to make, bees do not hole up in a little honeybee conference room and bust out PowerPoint presentations. They leave the hive to see what's out there in their surrounding environment.
- **Second, they come back together and engage in active, objective sharing of information.** There are no bee

spin doctors, no bee talking heads, no bee pundits. They come back to the hive and share what they've learned, openly, directly, and objectively.

• **Third, they reiterate this process** until the information is complete and compelling.

• **Finally, and most importantly, bees have a clear, shared common value system.** They all know what makes for the best hive location, and those are the criteria upon which their decisions are based.[1] There are no hidden agendas, no political motives—the bees just seek the best answer.

As Dr. Seeley talked, I felt more and more excited, and also, curiously, more and more at ease, a sense of ease I had not felt in a long time. I realized that the honeybees' characteristics are the exact same ones that lead to the best investment decisions.

The best investors I know go out into the world, observing, interacting, gathering information. They do not expect investment ideas to pop out of the screens on their desks; the best ideas come from the real world. And once they have an initial thought, great investors want to debate it, especially with others who might have different information. They are not concerned about pitching stocks or winning a sound-bite contest; they want to be challenged by other informed people who have different points of view. And finally, great investors have a clear, strong value system. It's so clear and so strong that they often don't even stop to think about it, but when they see an opportunity that is a match for their approach, for their own definition of good investing, it is clear as day.

I realized as Dr. Seeley spoke that the core of my profession was completely intact. In fact, it was beautifully aligned with the basic, brilliant principles that govern the natural world. It turned out that this struggle I felt was not against my vocation, the *profession* of investing—my struggle was against the *business* of investing, all of the tools and mechanics and distraction that we've created. These tools are each helpful in their own small ways, but their cumulative effect had been to gradually pull me off center, away from the essential, connected nature of investing.

So, I decided I needed to be more like a honeybee. To deliberately refocus on an investment approach that was more open, more connected to the world, and more explicitly focused on its guiding value system.

This re-rooting involved some change. I left the hive, the firm that I had loved, the professional home where I had thrived for almost twenty years. This was the place where I had taken on my first glamorous assignment fresh out of college, as a cement industry analyst. This was the place where I had managed my first sector fund, at the shocking age of twenty-two (never fear, I was very well supervised). This was the place where one company management team brought cake to our update meeting, because they knew I'd be working late on my birthday. This was the place where I'd managed billions of dollars, where I'd met countless CEOs and analyzed hundreds of businesses. This was the place where I'd taken on the toughest management role of all, managing an intense and brilliant team of people (much more challenging than managing money). In that hive, I had had more opportunity than I'd ever dreamed of, had worked side by side with some of the best investors of all time, had learned and been tested in every possible way, and, best of all, had forged many dear, lifelong friendships.

Leaving my home colony, needless to say, was both exciting and unsettling. I reengaged in the world around me, travelling as a volunteer and a pilgrim. I earned a degree at Harvard Divinity School, to strengthen my own core of values that underpin all decision making. And I started Honeybee Capital, with the simple premise that pollination of ideas, connection to the real world, and a strong underlying value system lead to optimal investment decisions.

Dr. Seeley's honeybees have now led me on a longer journey, a broader exploration of how all sorts of natural systems can provide us with road maps for our own human-created systems. Thanks to the generosity and vision of Janine Benyus and Hazel Henderson, who led a joint gathering of biomimicry leaders and investment innovators in 2011, ultimately my research has led to a deeper study of biomimicry, a framework for understanding the key characteristics of all natural systems and organisms. Applying the principles of biomimicry (life's principles) to investing gives us an approach that realigns and reintegrates our investment activity with the world around us.

The biomimicry-based framework offers several key advantages:

- **It is the ultimate in sustainability.** Nature has sustained for 3.8 billion years! In fact, it goes beyond sustainable: nature is adaptive and regenerative.

- **It is nonjudgmental.** Nature can be a wonderful instructor, but it is not preachy. Nature just *is*. Nature does not lecture you; nature demonstrates how the world actually functions.
- **It is an inherently integrated approach.** No single component of a natural system exists in isolation. Employing biomimicry automatically employs a networked, systems-based, integrated methodology.
- **It is inspiring and comforting.** Relying on deep, functional knowledge, embedded in ancient, real, observable natural systems, feels a lot better than taking up the latest clever (but limited) business school buzzwords. And the examples provided by nature are just stunning in their elegance and effectiveness.
- **It is flexible and durable.** Life's principles focus on adaptability, local responsiveness, and resource efficiency; they incorporate and anticipate all sorts of environments and changes. These are not ideas that become suddenly invalid when things shift. Just the opposite, they are even more illuminating in times of flux.
- **It is un-fluffy.** Nature is not all rainbows and kittens, and natural systems certainly do not sit in a romantic state of perpetual balance and bliss. It is the disruptions in nature, and the responses to them, that can teach us the most.

As I have employed these biomimicry principles more and more in my own investing, I have found greater clarity in my decision making, greater total returns (both financial and nonfinancial), and yes, greater joy. Investing according to life's principles has led me away from the overly engineered, disconnected, mechanical parts of finance. I still use many of those helpful tools, but they are now in their proper context: used as tools only, not as drivers of my decision making. And I've been able to refocus on the connected, integrated, mutually beneficial activity that represents investing in its truest and best form.

This is where real value is created. This is where our future lies. Biomimicry investing requires our most intellectually and emotionally robust resources. It requires us not to react blindly to numbers on a screen, but to engage proactively with the world around us. It requires us to utilize our full, independent, creative, multifaceted minds. It requires us, in the broadest and most inspiring way, to THINK.

The Roots of Biomimicry Investing

Two things fill the mind with ever new
and increasing wonder and awe:
the starry heavens above and the
moral law within.
—Immanuel Kant,
Critique of Practical Reason[1]

We are all investors. We invest our time, our energy, our money. We invest every single day, as citizens, as consumers, as businesspeople. At its core, done well, investing is well aligned with nature. It involves connection, exchange, and mutual benefit: we humans invented this activity, to serve our own needs, our communities, and our planet.

Lately, however, this primary, beneficial function of *investing* has become overshadowed by ever-more-extended iterations of *finance*. In my definition, finance consists of all of the secondary activity that's related to those initial exchanges: in its earlier stages finance produced vehicles like the stock market, where activity was still closely connected to the real world. You can buy stock in a railroad company, and assuming the price you pay is a fair one, if the railroad business does well, your investment will likely do well, too.

But as our tools have become more and more specialized, they've taken on a life of their own. We now have funds of funds, securitizations on top of securitizations, and entire firms whose businesses are based on harvesting the advantage of microseconds of trading speed. None of these developments is inherently bad, but each one pulls us further and further away from that primary, useful function of investing: flow of resources and mutually beneficial exchange. When we move deeper into the specialized mechanics of finance, we often end up in the realm of speculation, and lose sight of the primary role of investing.

Additionally, as risks and uncertainties have mounted in recent years, we've sought more control over our investing. The trouble is, driven by fear, we have focused on the wrong goals. Instead of aiming for resilient, optimized portfolios, we have sought risk-free, return-maximizing strategies that promise to sail through uncertain conditions unscathed. Or we've sought more safety, protection at any cost. These approaches might sound great, but they are figments. Fiction. Our faith in mechanics has become stronger than our faith in human judgment. Our faith in individual tools has become stronger than our faith in a connected whole. Our efforts to confine risk have just rearranged it into different pieces and different places, and in some cases magnified the dangers. We desperately seek control. But what we *need* is flexibility, adaptability, and resilience.

So what is the result of our intense focus on organization, mechanization, and risk management? In many ways it is the worst of all worlds, where risk and uncertainty are increasingly hidden, but undeniably present. Where flexibility and adaptation are constrained by ever smaller investment-style boxes and ever greater layers of processing (and cost) between the investor and the investment. Where our structures and systems are increasingly complicated, but without the benefits of variation and diversity. Where our investment products are more and more numerous, but controlled by fewer and fewer entities.

It is now widely recognized that our financial system is not as robust nor as resilient as we'd hoped and planned, and proposed reforms tend to focus on ever more complex regulation, with increasingly esoteric bureaucratic levers in the system. The premise is that if we make the rules dense and detailed enough, we will somehow be protected.

What my own journey as a professional investor has shown is that there is a time to "go deep" like this, to dive into more specialized pools of knowledge and tactics. However, there is also a time to "cut across," to look for other models that are not specialized, but rather more connected and universal. It may be appropriate to regulate the micro-level details of the financial *business*, but I also believe that the time has come for us to refocus on the investing *profession*. We need to reengage with investing in its essential, connected form—to reintegrate our profession with the real world, instead of the world on the screen.

How can we re-center our focus on investing in this original, beneficial role? Traditional economic theory, upon which traditional investment theory relies, can be useful, but it is incomplete. These theories take a mechanical approach, and to do so they must begin with a series of disconnects. One of the first phrases that any Econ101 student learns is "ceteris paribus," "all else constant." But "all else" is never constant. Likewise, a long list of "externalities" is ignored in all sorts of economic studies and business decisions, even when those externalities are vitally important, and not external at all. This does not make traditional economic theory useless, but, like any set of tools, we need to be conscious of its shortcomings.

Re-rooting investing is no small task. It requires a philosophical framework that is flexible enough to apply to many layers of a system, yet steady enough to apply to all sorts of shifting circumstances. It requires ideas that are aspirational, yet still easily linked to practice in the real world. It requires tools that are connected to deep truths and observable facts.

Biomimicry fits this bill. It is both philosophy and practice. A provocative, nuanced approach to transforming finance is to use biology instead of mechanical engineering as our starting point for modeling. Specifically, biomimicry provides us with a model that embodies connection and integration, a model of our natural systems that have proven to be effective, adaptive, and sustainable for 3.8 billion years. This is not a nifty new quantitative approach or a fancy consultant's pitch; the principles of biomimicry, life's principles, describe how the natural world actually functions. As educator Dayna Baumeister notes, "biomimicry is an emerging discipline of an ancient practice."[2]

This is not the newest theory. This is our most ancient wisdom. In my own search for a more complete, reconnected approach to investing, I was fortunate to find my mentors in biomimicry, Janine Benyus and Dayna Baumeister. The visionary futurist Hazel Henderson drew us together with other biomimicry and investing enthusiasts at a small gathering in 2011, and by noon on the first day I realized that, though we were deep in discussions about all that was flawed in our current world, I was breathing more deeply. I was wide awake. I was smiling. Unlike some sustainability frameworks, biomimicry does not root itself in anger and blame. It begins with acknowledging the reality of connected systems, and from that springs a natural and genuine sense of responsibility, stewardship, participation, and care. While a blame-centered approach begins with liability, shame, and negativity, a responsibility-centered approach begins with agency and positivity.[3]

As we sank into deeper and deeper conversation in Hazel's Florida backyard, I felt more than optimistic, more than hopeful. I felt a great sense of homecoming. I felt powerful. For the first time since I'd begun working in sustainable investing, I did not feel the need to convince anyone that I was right (or righteous). Janine and Dayna's work reminds us that this is how the entire natural world functions: it is our choice whether or not to align with nature's principles in the short term, but ultimately, they do prevail. There's a reason we say, "don't mess with Mother Nature."

This book's discussions of biomimicry and of life's principles draw heavily on the work of Janine and Dayna, on materials they've published, and on teaching and discussions that form the Biomimicry Specialist educational program.[4] It also builds upon the inspiring vision set forth in the *Principles of Ethical Biomimicry Finance,* authored primarily by Hazel, Janine, and Rosalinda Sanquiche after that initial gathering in Florida.[5] I offer these highlights, plus my own interpretations of their applications to investing, with tremendous gratitude to Janine, Dayna, Chris Allen, Hazel, Rosalinda, and all of our many colleagues throughout the years. Not only are these people brilliant and pioneering intellectuals, they are also generous and compassionate teachers and doers.

The Roots of Biomimicry Practice

In its simplest form, biomimicry is a straightforward practice. It's pausing before every creation, every decision, every design, and asking ourselves, "what would nature do here?" **WWND?** This phrase asks us to draw on the wisdom of nature before jumping to our preprogrammed, engineered default mechanisms. It opens us up to creativity and connection. The "here" adds an important nuance, reminding us that context is vital. We don't want to cut and paste convenient, random pieces of nature's guidance; we want to explore deep layers of wisdom within their appropriate context.

What nature would do is tangible; it is observable all around us. Perhaps that's why a long walk can be the best remedy for writer's block, or the best way to calm down after an anxious or angry encounter. Nature is sustainable; it is geared to optimize; it is inherently connected and regenerative. And because of all those things, it is aligned with the deepest human wisdom, whether from philosophers or spiritual leaders or indigenous communities. Or perhaps it is more appropriate to say that they are aligned with nature.

In its more complete application, biomimicry asks us to look to nature as **model, mentor, and measure**. As model, nature offers lessons from 3.8 billion years of sustainability. We can use these lessons to innovate our own products and processes to be more in alignment with life's principles. As mentor, nature provides us with wisdom, not just raw materials. And as measure, nature offers clear tests for

whether any endeavor meets standards of truly long-term, full-cycle, integrated sustainability. To these three, I would also add **"muse,"** as I have seen firsthand how much creativity can be unleashed by simply observing the wonders living all around us.

Biomimicry is also inherently a **multilayered approach**: the same framework can be applied to forms, processes, and entire systems. This makes it perfect for applying to a multidimensional area like investing, where one of our biggest challenges has been the development of tools and languages that are ultra-specific to small pieces of the field, without linking back to the whole.

Similarly, biomimicry is **scale agnostic**: it can be applied at micro, meso, macro, and meta levels. In my work I use biomimicry to look at individual companies, my own investment processes, investment products and tools, and the entire financial system. The contexts are specific and varied, but the principles are universal.

Here's What Biomimicry Is Not

Biomimicry is not an overly romanticized view of the world and its functions. Nature is not just sunshine and puppies; it is also hurricanes and vipers, droughts and rats. We can learn from the darkness of nature as well as its light. Nature demonstrates systemic principles that are often different from the ones used in human-created systems, and natural systems also adjust to change and disruption differently (and usually better) than human-created systems. There are frequent, large disruptions and imbalances in nature, but throughout all of that, life strives to create conditions conducive to life. We can learn from these disruptions and adaptations as much as (and maybe even more than) from an ongoing healthy system.

Perhaps most important, biomimicry is not just copying nature, like the mechanical hummingbirds recently developed by DARPA. It is not pasting nature into nonnatural environments, like adding bamboo flooring to a high-rise in the desert. And it is not simply employing nature as if it were a subcontractor, taking bits and pieces that are useful to us, without regard for context, process, or system. **Biomimicry focuses on embracing nature's wisdom, not extracting nature's stuff.** This starting point is one of open inquiry and curiosity—asking "how" instead of "how much."

Getting Started

Since biomimicry is scientifically rooted, it is tempting to jump right in with our linear minds, to begin analyzing its principles, implementing its practices, following its checklists straightaway. And yet to be most effective, there are three essential, qualitative points of orientation needed before we begin.

First, **rearrange**: nature is not separate from us—**we are nature**. This idea is obvious and yet sadly unfamiliar, because we are often conditioned to think of nature "over there." Even some of our most ardent environmental movements are premised on the need to save the whales, or the rainforest, or the spotted owl, as if these elements are distant from ourselves, when in fact they are all part of our own larger, connected ecosystem. Sometimes the notion of human agency leads us to stay stuck in a disconnected state, thinking we are acting "for" or "against" instead of "with" our fellow creatures.

The second orientation point is the recognition of how investing and finance fit into our broader world. Especially for those of us engaged in investing professionally, the financial markets can sometimes take on a life of their own. They seem like primary drivers of our own lives, of the economy, and of our societies, when in reality, of course, finance is just one smallish subset of our total activity. **Reframing** investing as just a fragment of human endeavor, and reframing human endeavor as a fragment of our natural environment, is a necessary task—and a humbling one.

The third adjustment has been trickiest of all for me: **refrain.** For many years, like lots of us, I've been trained to be as quick and clever as possible, especially in professional settings. And when I am exposed to an exciting new idea, these tendencies are all the more heightened. I want to solve the puzzle, fast. I want to win. But for effective biomimicry practice, we need to **quiet our cleverness.** In order to learn from nature, we need to observe with an open mind-set, without actively seeking an answer right away.

This quiet-mindedness has similarities to "beginner's mind" in meditation practices, where even experienced practitioners are encouraged to approach their practice with openness and equanimity. This same concept is present in some of our best investment practices, since any investor who hunts with too narrow a focus for opportunities is sure to miss out in two ways. First, she'll miss anything that is outside of her narrowed-down scope of vision. And second, she will be tempted to force false conclusions from that small data set. Without some sense of the broader context, some sense of how the micro fits with the macro, a sound decision is impossible. This is not to imply that there is no need for focus, but to emphasize that that focus must be undertaken *after* gaining an understanding of the surrounding environment.

Perhaps this kind of indirect beginning sounds a little *too* patient—after all, our challenges are urgent! But it's not so difficult or time consuming to get started. Here are the simple instructions:

Go outside.
Breathe deep.
Again.
Try to look—without searching.
Try to listen—without hunting.
Wait—just a little while.
Then begin.

PART II

Re-Rooting Investing: Six Transformations

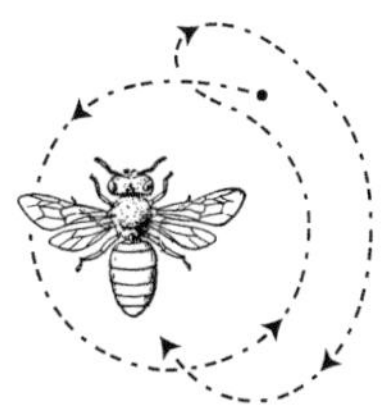

Transformation 1

From Efficient to Effective

Several years ago, I sat down with my parents to review their investments as they planned for retirement. There was nothing too crazy to discuss—they held no hidden Cayman Island accounts, no illiquid private equity funds, no time-shares in the Everglades. But there was a lot of complication for what was a simple savings plan: no fewer than eight different forms of government-backed savings vehicles, plus a long list of mutual funds that all mainly invested in large U.S. companies. Over the years, each time there was a chance to save a little more, my parents were guided to a new opportunity, and each opportunity was perfectly reasonable. But after forty years of new opportunities, rather than diversification, my folks had a lot of needless duplication. Just as importantly, they had account statements from all sorts of institutions coming out of their ears, which meant a lot of time and energy were required just to keep all of their records straight.

I see the same tendencies in my own consumption patterns, a sort of unintentional and unnecessary stockpiling. My cupboard often contains multiple cans of tomatoes, just because I can't recall what's there. My closet contains no fewer than ten black T-shirts, just because the newest one seems a little better or different. My portfolio summary lists dozens of stocks, just because each seems unique and intriguing. If these choices add something valuable—whether it's better fashion choices or the enjoyment of learning about new companies—that's fine. But in many cases, like my parents', more does not mean better. When it comes to investing, what we need is not more complication, or false variety. We need deeper efficiency—true effectiveness.

Nature's Principle: Be Resource and Energy Efficient

If there's one thing Wall Street is supposed to have right, it's efficiency. As recently as the early 1990s, just having the fastest fax machines or the bandwidth to receive real-time stock quotes could be a big advantage to an investor. Now, just twenty years later, those forms of efficiency seem quaint: large firms spend billions of dollars for ultra-fast trading systems, there are text crawlers that can automatically flag phrases like "lower guidance" or "higher revenues" in press releases, and I have seven different apps that provide me with real-time stock quotes right here on my phone. But efficiency is not just about speed, and it's not just about cost. "Fast and cheap" is a common but shallow form of efficiency, one that feels good in the short term, but ultimately has hidden costs.

The natural principle, **be resource efficient,** reflects a much more nuanced, much deeper form. In nature, efficiency includes sophisticated design principles, like multifunctionality, and fitting form to function. Natural efficiency is not the same as a quick fix; it is true effectiveness. The subprinciples of resource efficiency are:

- Use multifunctional design.
- Use low-energy processes.
- Recycle all materials.
- Fit form to functions.

For example, have you ever seen a duck preening itself beside a pond? I have to admit, it never seemed a remarkable sight to me, until I learned about the amazing design elements of the duck's preen oil. This oil is amazing stuff, and a great illustration of the subprinciple of **multifunctional design**: it is produced by the duck's own body, can be used for both feather waterproofing and duck-bill moisturizing, and it breaks down into vitamin D when exposed to sunlight. This oil is not just an efficient product by shallow standards (fast and cheap); it is *effective*, performing many functions with simple, internally sourced materials.[1]

A perfect illustration of the second efficiency subprinciple, **use low-energy processes**, is the toco toucan. The toucan's bill serves many purposes, and one of the most interesting is as a heat exchanger. When it's colder, the toucan reduces blood flow to its bill, keeping more of that heat inside. And when it's warmer, blood flow increases, allowing more heat to escape through the large surface area of the bill. The toucan does not need to flap its wings to get warm or seek out an external, high-energy cooling mechanism: this adjustment all happens internally, and efficiently.[2]

The third subprinciple in this section, **recycle all materials,** is well demonstrated by the hermit crab, source of many childhood nightmares for me (click...clack...click). If I'd known about the principles of resource efficiency, at least I could have put that sleepless time to good use, thinking about how effective the hermit crab is in finding its home. Hermit crabs are the squatters of the seaside scene: they find an empty shell and move right in. But they don't take just any shell: their behavior is influenced by both what's available and by the condition of their current dwelling. Shells are recycled constantly, in a way that maximizes benefit.[3] Maybe they are not as flashy as the big-billed toucan, but the crabs illuminate resource-efficiency principles just as the birds do.

The final subprinciple related to efficiency, **fit form to functions,** is elegantly embodied in all sorts of organisms, such as the cactus species *lophophora*. This type of cactus is designed to shrink when water is scarce, so much so that its shoots flatten out and retract all the way underground. Then when water is available, the shoots pop back up again aboveground. The form is perfectly designed to fit the essential function of water management.[4]

As we translate the principles of resource efficiency from biological settings to a human setting, it's important to note three fundamental concepts that are embedded within the directive to "be resource efficient." First, **form and function go hand in hand, and are based on need.** Performing unnecessary functions is, by definition, not efficient, since there is no meaningful benefit produced. And providing function with a mismatched form is wasteful, using more energy and resources than are truly required. Say you have two forms of transportation—your feet and a sailboat. And you have two destinations—the corner store and a remote island. Well, none of these components is inherently "good" or "bad"—but the combination of your feet and the trip to the corner store obviously matches form and function, whereas it would waste a lot of energy to try to walk (or swim) to that island. Behind every function is a need, and for every function there is a form. If it's a really good form, it fits numerous functions with one design.

The second underlying idea is the **relationship between efficiency and effectiveness**. Sometimes things that are efficient are also effective, like the toucan's bill or cactus shoots. But sometimes we are so focused on shallow, low-level definitions of efficiency—like speed—that we fall far short of the mark for deep, true effectiveness. For example, there is a small restaurant on Charles Street in Boston where seating is very limited. Instead of everyone rushing for the few empty chairs, the managers ask that you stand in line, order, and only take a seat once you have your food. This small adjustment is deeply uncomfortable for many customers: you can see the furrowed brows, the glances over shoulders, the occasional coat draped over a chair despite a large sign noting the seating policy. The desire to save a seat *now* is powerful, even though it's not tied to an immediate need. This wait-and-sit approach seems inefficient but it is truly effective: there are exactly the right number of seats available at exactly the right time, resulting in near–100 percent occupancy. True, the seating process is not super-speedy. This is a more profound form of efficiency, optimizing time, space, and expense.

The final embedded concept is one of **duration.** Efficiency in a natural context takes a full-cycle, multidimensional view, unlike many human endeavors. If a new manufacturing process uses less material, but is much more energy intensive and leaves toxic by-products at the end, it is not in alignment with the resource-efficiency principle. Managing across many dimensions and multiple time frames is harder, for sure. To align fully with this principle we need to include elegant, multifunctional design; material and energy efficiency; recycled and recyclable materials; and fitting form to functions. This is a much more daunting task than just aiming for "cheap right now." But if it's harder, so what? As Jack Welch has said, we need to eat, and we need to dream.[5] Or to quote my mom, "Honey, that's why they call it work. It's supposed to be hard." Aiming for deep effectiveness does not offer shortcuts or partial credit: we need to embrace the nuance as much as the headline. We are all already functioning effectively across numerous settings, every day; as citizens, as businesspeople, as artists, as innovators, as family members, and yes, as investors. These natural principles acknowledge that multidimensional reality, and extend it into more realms of practice.

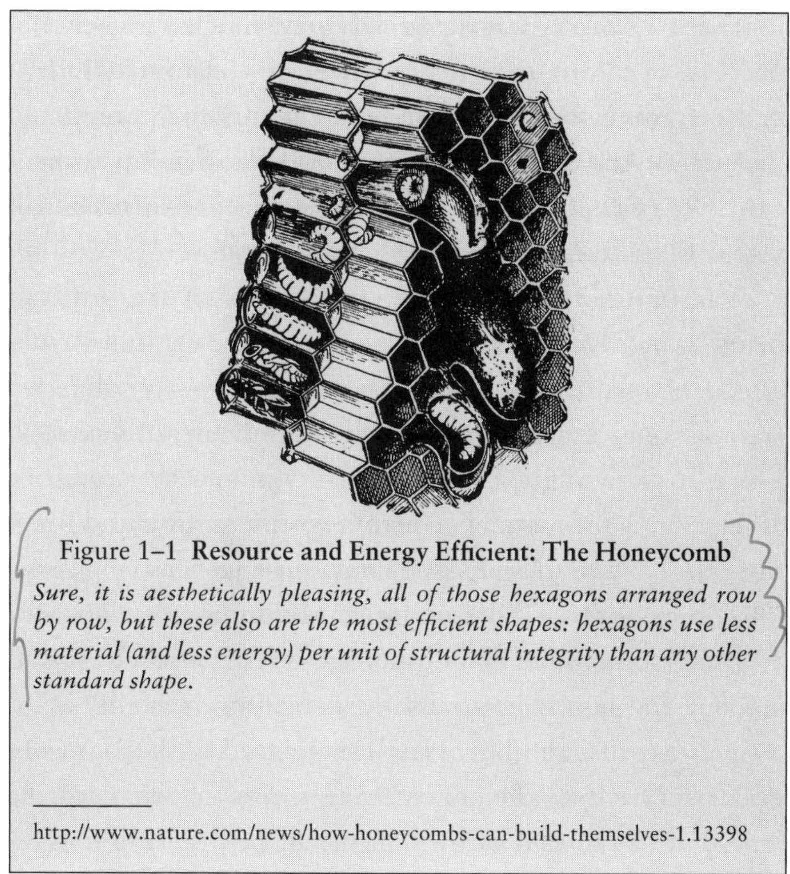

Figure 1–1 **Resource and Energy Efficient: The Honeycomb**

Sure, it is aesthetically pleasing, all of those hexagons arranged row by row, but these also are the most efficient shapes: hexagons use less material (and less energy) per unit of structural integrity than any other standard shape.

http://www.nature.com/news/how-honeycombs-can-build-themselves-1.13398

Translation to Investing

It's tempting to claim that resource-efficient investing is already alive and well. For each of the efficiency subprinciples, plenty of financial illustrations come easily to mind. Take the fundamental building block of money—it is certainly multifunctional, able to serve as a store of wealth, a measure of transaction value, and, in hyperinflationary periods, as wallpaper. Additionally, there is almost no cost to trade securities these days—so surely that is a low-energy process. Speaking of securities, we are constantly trading and retrading the same ones—this seems to be recycling materials. And there are so many forms that investment can take, well, surely we can argue that its forms fit all sorts of functions.

Oh, but there's the key. Function. What is the function of investing? What is its purpose? What constitutes truly *effective* investing—beyond a fast-and-cheap, shallow, transactional efficiency? What would an investment look like if it were aligned with all of the nuances of resource efficiency? A mismatch between investment form and function can have vivid and significant consequences.

For example, who can forget the famous *Good Will Hunting* scene, where Will out-quotes the obnoxious grad student and notes that the same education is available for a small expense in library late fees instead of thousands of dollars in tuition. The grad student sneers that that may be true, but at the end of his education, he'll have a degree, unlike Will.[6] And there you have it, the mega-question. What is the function of investing in education? To be educated, or to have a degree? If it's the former, Will's approach—investing time—is obviously the best fit, and the grad student is foolish to spend all that money. But if the degree is what's valued instead, then those many-thousand-dollar tuition payments might indeed be a resource-efficient path.

So the real question we ask needs to include both **function and context:** *what is the purpose of investing in this situation?* For individuals, this can sometimes be answered in simple monetary terms, like, "I need income of $5000 per year from this investment." Or it can be answered in multifaceted terms, such as, "I want to support my local agricultural community, and I need this money back in two years." In some cases these answers reveal more complex personal priorities, like, "I need this money to buy a house someday, but I want to honor my aunt who was an anti-war protester, so I'd like to invest in a way that promotes peace." You can see why we often avoid this kind of nuance in defining investment function: it's much more difficult! But it's more interesting, more true to life, and ultimately it can be more rewarding.

For investment professionals, the context may be different from an individual investor's, and the answers may be even tougher to come by. If your firm is introducing a new investment fund, why? What need is it fulfilling? If the purpose is to grow your own business, that's fine—just say so, and settle the surrounding questions of form and process accordingly. If the purpose is to provide a new or different service to your clients, why is that new service needed? What sort of form best fits that purpose? Perhaps the appropriate form is partnership with other providers, or use of processes that already exist elsewhere, rather than expending energy and expense in creating your own offerings.

Many of the biggest mistakes in the history of finance are rooted in misstated or made-up statements of need. Who needed tulip bulbs in 1637? Hardly anyone—or at least far fewer than the number who *wanted* tulip bulbs, which led to tulip mania and the subsequent crash, all out of alignment with principles of efficiency and effectiveness.

Note that the definition of need is not required to be noble or righteous—just clear and true. And, most importantly, the needs can vary—there is not one single purpose for investing, nor should there be.

With a clearly identified need, it becomes much easier to find forms that fit, to see which materials will be best suited for the task at hand, and to ensure efficient, multifunctional design of investing approaches. Understanding **purpose** is the root of what takes us from merely fast and cheap to deeply efficient and effective.

Natural Scorecard: Investment Helpers

I've been thinking about these questions of purpose with respect to my parents and their retirement savings. If, at each step of the way, we were able to clearly assess need, form, and function, we would be unlikely to end up with a dozen different retirement accounts (or a dozen cans of tomatoes), all performing the same essential function. In the case of my folks, luckily, the duplication was benign: it added complication, but not significant cost or risk. But that's not true for many investors, who often encounter waves of complications that have great big price tags attached.

Consider a plain-vanilla solution for many investors, the mutual fund. An actively managed fund has average fees of about seventy-seven basis points (bp) a year; this means you pay 0.77 percent of your money—$7.70 for every $1000 you're investing—to the manager every year, whether performance is up, down, or sideways. An index fund is much lower cost, only thirteen basis points annually, but still, there is a fee.[7] And what do you get for this fee? Well, you get professionals looking after your assets. You get accurate accounting and tax records. You get peace of mind knowing that others are worrying about the financial markets on your behalf. Alas, you do *not* get superior performance, at least not automatically; across all equity and fixed income categories, less than 50 percent of actively managed mutual funds have outperformed their benchmarks on a ten-year basis, and in some categories as many as 80 percent of funds underperform.[8]

Still, this might seem like a pretty fair trade—good service, diversification, and at least the possibility of superior returns, in exchange for modest fees. How does the mutual fund investment option stack up against the principles of resource efficiency?

- **Does it use multifunctional design?** Well, there is one major function—to act as an effective vehicle for investing—and mutual funds are well designed for that. Plus, you can use the same fund design for all sorts of investing—stocks, bonds, different regions, different-sized companies. But these functions are all very closely related—it's not like preen oil for the duck, where it's a moisturizer and water repellant and nutrient all in one.
- **Does it employ low-energy processes?** Pretty much—compared with investing your own time and energy, or much more complex investment schemes, mutual funds stack up pretty well. They are easy to use, and are adaptable with little extra energy required to adjust.

• **Are all materials recycled?** Hmm, in some ways. Components of mutual funds (individual stocks and bonds) are constantly being bought and sold, reconfigured in different combinations to produce full investment portfolios.

• **Does it fit form to functions?** Fairly well—the form is simple and fairly flexible. You can use it to invest in all sorts of different securities, and for all sorts of reasons. But these functions are all closely linked, as noted above.

In short, the answer to all of these questions is somewhere around a B or B minus. Simple mutual funds are aligned with resource-efficient principles, but in a pretty narrow way.

However, for many these days, mutual funds are considered child's play—too basic for real, serious investors with real, serious investment objectives. Warren Buffett famously wrote about these investors and their waves of "helpers" in his 2005 annual report (that section of his report is titled, "How to Minimize Investment Returns," so you can see where this is headed). Buffett tells of the fictional Gotrocks family, approached in succession by different sorts of financial helpers. First come the broker-helpers, followed by manager-helpers, followed by consultant-helpers, followed by hyper-helpers. Each layer of helper may be well intentioned, and may provide some value, but each also adds cost to the Gotrocks' investment process, and in many cases this cost is far in excess of value received.[9] This concern applies to institutional investors and their advisors as well as individuals.[10]

This might seem like a minor issue—what's a few basis

points in fees, especially if they bring added expertise and sound judgment to your investment process? Let's add it up. Here is a quick and simple summary of the costs of complication for investors:

- **Index fund**—just a mirror of securities that are in a particular index. Cost = 13 bp.
- **Actively managed** equity mutual fund—"stockpicking" approach, a subset of securities that aims to outperform the relevant index. Cost = 77 bp.[11]
- **Fund of funds** product—a bundle of different funds, usually with an extra layer of fees. Cost = 91 bp.[12]
- **Hedge funds**—a particular kind of fund that has more investment freedom, and thus hopefully more chance to perform well. Cost = typically "2 and 20," or 200 bp annually, plus 20 percent of gains.
- **Investment advisors**—someone to help decide amongst the thousands of options available, with the aim of tailoring decisions to your own situation. Cost = 106 bp annually, on top of all of the product-specific fees noted above.[13]

This list does not include the even more convoluted options that are often used by high-net-worth individuals or institutions: funds of hedge funds, extra layers of investment consultants, and so on. And these fees are all annual fees, paid not just once, but every single year, regardless of performance.

There are plenty of times when these sorts of fees are justified: long-term investment performance could be great, or perhaps an investor really needs and values the assistance of an advisor. Perhaps you are investing for reasons that go beyond financial goals—such as improving the local food web or supporting new entrepreneurs—and the nonfinancial information and results that these advisors help to provide are well worth the fees involved. For the record, for many years I was a portfolio manager of actively managed equity mutual funds, and our goal was always to beat market (and thus index) performance, *after* accounting for all fees. As the chairman of our company used to say, "We are not here for our own amusement." People were counting on us to steward their hard-earned savings in a responsible and effective manner. So the point is not simply to conclude "Fees are bad," but rather to ask the more important questions, "What function is served by these fees? What value do they reflect?"

Even if great value is provided, the costs of investment fees can be tremendous. Say you invest $100,000 in an index fund for ten years at a fee of thirteen bp per year ($130 in fees for year one). If returns are 5 percent per year, at the end of the decade you have about $161,000—a total return for the decade of 61 percent. However, if you invest that same $100,000 in a hedge fund, your fees are two hundred bp ($2000 in year one), plus 20 percent of investment gains. If returns are 5 percent per year, the same as the index fund, at the end of the decade you have $122,000, a total return of just 22 percent for the whole decade. Put another way, because of the higher fees, returns in the hedge fund need to be about 8.5 percent per year in order for you to end up with the same amount of money as owning the index fund with performance of 5 percent. At the 5 percent performance level, you have paid $39,000 in additional fees over that time period for the hedge fund structure.

This quick exercise shows why road maps like natural principles are so useful—because our minds are not well suited to considering ripple effects and compounding.[14] Even if we intellectually understand the facts about layers of fees, and even if we are great at doing compound math in our heads, 2 or 3 percent sounds small. Here's the thing: a 3 percent chance of rain means near-certain sun, but a 3 percent investment fee could set you up for terrible storms. Our brains have a hard time distinguishing between these two very different contexts for "3 percent."

An assessment of an "ultra-helped" investment model—one that uses complicated products and layers of advisors—against the principles of resource efficiency shows how it comes up short:

- **Does it use multifunctional design?** This sort of arrangement still serves the major function of investing, but it uses more and more products and inputs to serve the same purpose; this is the opposite of multifunctional design.
- **Does it employ low-energy processes?** As increasingly processed investments and more layers of advisors are added, energy use increases.
- **Are all materials recycled?** As with our mutual fund example, you could say that the components of these funds

are often traded and reconfigured, but this remains a pretty narrow interpretation of "recycling."

- **Does it fit form to functions?** The hyper-helped investing model is inherently more complicated than a simpler approach, and there is little evidence that it performs the essential investing functions better. This seems to be a situation of overengineering rather than a simple, elegant match of form to function.

As noted above, there are times when a complicated, multilayered investment approach might make sense, when it matches a similarly multilayered set of needs. But much of the time, this sort of highly engineered approach adds a lot of cost and complication while providing extra features that are not especially relevant, valued, or needed.

Here we come to an important distinction: **complicated versus complex**. In this context, the words mean very different things. A complicated system, or a complicated investment product, is just one that is hard to manage, or hard to explain. It's difficult, but it's predictable. A complex system, on the other hand (more precisely, a complex adaptive system), is comprised of heterogeneous, connected parts that interact with one another in unpredictable ways and change over time. Therefore, the whole system cannot be described just by summing up the individual pieces; as a collective, the system shows emergent properties that make it hard to link cause and effect in a simple, linear way.[15] Think of a beehive: each bee is performing tasks that are describable, definable, and maybe even predictable. But adding up the actions of each individual bee does not even begin to describe the function of the entire hive. A group of individual bees is complicated; a whole hive of bees working together is complex.

There are two reasons why this difference between complicated and complex is so important for thinking about effective investment practices. First, we often take a simple need and match it with a complicated solution or product. Someone just wants to save money for college tuition and before you know it, they are invested through three layers of advisors in a fund of funds, paying 2 percent in fees, when they could fulfill the same essential purpose for one-tenth the cost. The solution is overengineered when compared with the simple function that is required.

Second, we often mistake complex situations for complicated ones. This sort of mistake can be more than costly; it can be devastating. These days we often do have genuinely complex investment needs: trying to mitigate risk for a big global portfolio that has ever-changing and unpredictable correlations within it, for example. We have tried to address *complex* purposes like this one by just throwing more *complicated* solutions at it. That's like performing highly technical heart valve surgery on someone who has a broken heart of an entirely different sort. Neat technology. Same general location. Totally wrong application. You will never solve the problem this way, just like you will never understand a beehive by watching individual bees. The form does not fit the function.

Evolution

Fortunately, there are increasing examples of reconnecting investing needs with simple, elegant, direct solutions. For example, peer-to-peer lending eliminates several layers of intermediaries by allowing more direct forms of loan making. To be sure, this comes with different characteristics than a neatly bundled-up investment product, including different risks, but it also offers more direct connection between investor and investee, which might well make it more aligned with the principles of resource and energy efficiency. Think about it—all of the resources saved by not having three or four sets of institutions involved in bundling up the loan (low-energy processes), a platform that can serve the needs of many different lenders and borrowers at once (multifunctional design), and a directness that allows for straightforward and simple transactions (fit form to function). The modern incarnations of peer-to-peer lending are in their infancy, but these are really new tools that extend an old concept, one seen in villages and religious communities and amongst friends and family for centuries. It's the idea of lending to people you know, combining financial risk with social assets, in a way that contributes to your own community. Simple, elegant forms of investing.

Other examples of effectiveness can be found in the field of impact investing. Because impact investors are actively seeking multidimensional returns (beyond just financial returns), established investment "boxes" don't always fit.

Consequently, many endeavors end up being very difficult to manage, with reams of legal paperwork and creative but complicated structures. However, organizations like RSF Social Finance, the Calvert Foundation, and TriLinc Global are offering investment options that streamline those piles of paperwork, meeting multiple functions (financial benefit, social benefit, community connection) in a way that aims to be less complicated, less costly, and more effective for their investors.

Pathway to Practice

What is real efficiency? It's not just cheap and fast. Deep efficiency—natural efficiency—includes complete views across a system and across a life cycle. Instead of asking whether an investment is easy to make, back up and ask, what purpose is this investment serving, and what form best matches that purpose? Then look around and ask, am I duplicating this function? If so, am I adding meaningful diversity, or just expending extra energy and resources by doing the same thing twice?

Once we're comfortable asking these questions about a specific investment, we can extend them to consider investing in its broader form. What are the key functions of *all* of your investing, whether you're investing time, money, or energy? Are the forms you've chosen efficient in a deep way, or just fast and cheap? Are there more creative solutions than the ones you've chosen, solutions that perform multiple functions and use fewer resources?

Our current investment culture values efficiency, but often we think of its shallowest form, merely quick and inexpensive. We can reorient this value toward its deeper form of true, systemic efficiency—real effectiveness.

If we've been solving investment puzzles by just trying to run faster, or by throwing more and more resources at the same type of solution (as in our ultra-helper model), we can pause to reconsider. What is the real intention of our activity? What functions are we trying to perform? And what forms best match those functions? Perhaps a simpler, more truly efficient form is all that we need, despite the allure of new layers and innovations.

In the end, my parents' choice of plain old Treasury bills and certificates of deposit at their local bank served their purpose quite well for many years, and did so in a simple, resource-efficient way. These investments did not make for good cocktail-party chatter; they are dull as dirt. But my folks were clear on the function they wanted to perform. They just wanted to save some money for retirement, not to engage layers of helpers, not to invest in currency swaps or Brazilian real estate, not to have cool stories to tell their friends. That clarity, and the efficient match of form and functions, has stood them in good stead.

Sowing Seeds of Resource-Efficient Investing

Here are some simple ideas to start us along a deeply efficient path:

- **Clarify the underlying functions** performed by your investments: is it financial return? What sort? What time frame? Is it other sorts of return? Social benefit, community building, personal or organizational connections? Nature does not falsely settle on a single function, and neither should we.

- **Acknowledge that more help and more resource intensity aren't always needed—or even beneficial.** Many of our investment processes include an embedded assumption that more is always better—bigger teams, more expertise, greater infrastructure. But natural systems use the *appropriate* level of resources and energy, not the maximum. Sometimes the appropriate level of complication is high, but often it is low.
- **Invest with a goal of fitting form to functions.** Aim for a clear match of form and function, not the fanciest, most innovative, most clever, or most popular possibility.

By more fully acknowledging the importance of resource and energy efficiency in our investments, we can identify the investment equivalent of the duck's preen oil or the toucan's bill. We can eliminate needless complexity and focus our energies on areas where the extra effort is needed and beneficial.

We can move from shallow efficiency to deep effectiveness.

Transformation 2

From Synthetic to Simple

"We have a great new product," my friend, a financial advisor, announced. "It's a synthetic market-hedging security, constructed so that if the market goes down, your losses are limited, but if the market goes up, you capture all of the gains."

Chatting at a coffee break, this conversation seemed innocent enough, but it came on the heels of the gigantic derivatives losses of 2008 and 2009, so everyone's risk antennae were up. My advisor friend (I'll call him Joe) fielded every question with grace and confidence and highly technical language. Still, this security clearly sounded too good to be true, so I asked the question I always ask when someone proposes seemingly magical models to me: "When will this not work?"

To his credit, Joe was well informed, and highlighted two important caveats: first, these mechanics only worked within certain bands of market performance, so if things were extremely bad or extremely good, the construction of the securities' performance did not hold. Second, these securities could not easily be sold, because once set up for a specific time period, they had to run their course, and could not be undone. The idea behind this offering was not a bad one, but it was very specific, managing a particular range of risk for a particular market for a particular time period.

Somehow as we talked, the image of processed cheese popped into my head. I grew up near Philadelphia, so trust me, I understand the value of Cheez Whiz, especially when properly applied to a steak sandwich or perhaps a soft pretzel. But everyone knows Cheez Whiz is not exactly the centerpiece of a healthy nutritional plan. In fact, one thing I admire about Cheez Whiz is the "z"—there is truth in that letter. This product doesn't even pretend to be actual cheese. We could use a labeling equivalent like this in the investment world—fundz of fundz, maybe, or derivativz—some signal that the product in question is not quite natural.

In the absence of such a label, we can employ the principles of nontoxic production.

Nature's Principle: Nontoxic Production

By now, we've all heard about "toxic securities," the ones that are unsellable, and seem to be worth less than zero. But what is the source of this toxicity? We don't often think of investing as a manufacturing business, but in fact all investments involve some sort of creation. Therefore, the means of creation are a vital component of a healthy financial system. If you are manufacturing auto parts and your goal is to have no toxic waste, you need to design that into the process from the very beginning. The same is true for finance.

To address these questions of healthy creation, we have nature's principles of **life-friendly chemistry**, which emphasize nontoxic production. The subprinciples in this category are:

- Do chemistry in water.
- Build selectively with a small subset of elements.
- Break down into benign constituents.

At first glance, this principle is a tough one to apply to social systems like investing: after all, in nature, chemistry is a literal, tangible thing. But even when studying natural systems, the word "chemistry" tends to throw some people off: we are talking about biology, right? So why all of this focus on chemistry and toxicity?

Well, at the molecular level, all that happens in the world is chemistry—whether it's in the forest or in the test tube. Assembling and combining elements produces a huge range of functions that are important in nature as well as in manufactured products—characteristics like color, structure, and strength. So when we think about the concept of nontoxic production, we mean that products in nature are assembled in a way that does not harm life.

Comparing the production processes in nature with the ones in human factories turns up some startling differences. There are no solvents in nature, no highly synthesized reagents, no dyes made of rare elements. Just as importantly, when natural organisms break down, we are left with benign, simple elements like carbon and nitrogen. There are no toxic dumps in nature.

For example, those amazing colors in peacock feathers? They are not colors at all, at least not the way we commonly think of color. The pigment in those feathers is actually brown. It's the structure of the feathers that reflects light to display all of those brilliant blues and greens. Small crystal-like structures are arranged to reflect and filter different wavelengths of light. There are no synthetic chemical compositions or artificial dyes required.[1]

Some might argue that humans have more complicated needs than natural systems (never mind that we are part of nature ourselves). We need to build tall buildings, for example, and how could you do that without steel? Well, spider webs are stronger than steel, with the proteins made completely "in house"—inside the spider. There is no need for two-thousand-degree furnaces. This isn't to deny steel's value to the world, but rather to illustrate that nature produces equally amazing products using a very simple subset of elements in elegant ways.

The subprinciples of healthy production add more nuance to this core concept: first, **do chemistry in water**. This is the "how" of nontoxic production, and reflects the fact that nature does not have the luxury of dumping synthetic reagents into the middle of its processes, nor does it have a warehouse full of synthesized, complex materials at its disposal. For example, tiny diatoms are among the most abundant organisms on earth, found almost anywhere that there is light and water. By some estimations, the photosynthesis of these simple creatures accounts for over 20 percent of the planet's oxygen production. One unique feature of diatoms is that their cell walls contain a large proportion of silica, which keeps their shapes remarkably consistent. When these walls are assembled, it's through the employment of specific proteins; essentially the diatom creates glass walls internally, with proteins—no need for a huge, energy-intensive furnace.[2]

If the first subprinciple relates to "how," the second one answers "what": **build selectively with a small subset of elements**. When we look at the periodic table, it gives each element equal space, equal weight on the chart. But in the reality of the natural world, the elements are anything but evenly distributed. Almost every beginning chemistry student has memorized the acronym CHON, because the vast bulk of natural organisms' mass is made up of just four elements: carbon, hydrogen, oxygen, and nitrogen. The next bundle of common elements includes calcium, chlorine, magnesium, potassium, phosphorous, sodium, and sulfur. And after that, the whole alphabet soup of the rest of the periodic table—well, those elements are really pretty rare. In the human body, for instance, 96 percent of our mass is made up of oxygen, carbon, hydrogen, and nitrogen.[3]

Once any product has been assembled, the next logical question is, "what then?" The answer is the subprinciple, **break down into benign constituents.** This concept is quite specific, demanding that decomposition results in no harmful by-products. However, it does *not* say that there are no toxic elements along the way. Take cobra venom, for example, an obviously toxic substance that still manages to be in alignment with life's principles. The venom is assembled without synthetic reagents, from simple elements, and then it breaks down into benign constituents. In between those stages, it performs its intended purpose—a highly toxic purpose (at least for the prey). The venom ensures protection and function for the snake in a spectacularly effective way, but with no toxic elements leftover at the end of the process.[4]

When we consider the application of these specific scientific ideas to human social settings, two important themes emerge. First, **this kind of production is not just simple—it is elegant.** When I look out the window and see the woods in the distance, dozens of types of trees and shrubs and living organisms, it seems miraculous that the ingredient list for that huge variety of life is so short. This is a key subtlety within the second subprinciple: not only is there a small subset of elements, but they are assembled in elegant, even exquisite, ways. It's like a master pastry chef who can fill a whole bakery with different arrangements of flour, butter, eggs, sugar, and yeast. A little salt here, a little vanilla there, maybe an occasional dash of cardamom or cinnamon, and voilà! Immense variety, produced with a tiny subset of ingredients plus elegant assembly techniques. Compare this vision of a gorgeous organic bakery with a stroll down the shelf-stable bakery aisle at the grocery store, where each label is less pronounceable than the last, and this abstract life's principle is suddenly crystal clear.

One misperception we often hold is that something simple, elegant, and benign is also somehow limited. This is the second vital concept that relates to nontoxic chemistry: **life-friendly processes are not limiting, or lesser.** To be fair, many of us have worn scratchy natural-fiber shirts or eaten leaden whole-grain muffins. But these shortcomings are problems of design and assembly, not shortcomings of natural components. As we can see from the toxicity of cobra's venom, the strength of spider's silk, the variety of the forest, and the elegance of the diatom, life-friendly chemistry does not mean "weak." It does not mean "plain." It does mean that we can create variety and function and splendor in a way that is conducive to life, instead of harmful.

We've been conditioned to think that limits are inherently bad, that they are something to be transcended, that every barrier should be broken. Janine Benyus notes, "We humans regard limits as a universal dare."[5] But limits at the start of a process—to the number or type of inputs, or to the conditions surrounding a problem and its solutions—do not necessarily limit the creativity of outputs. In fact,

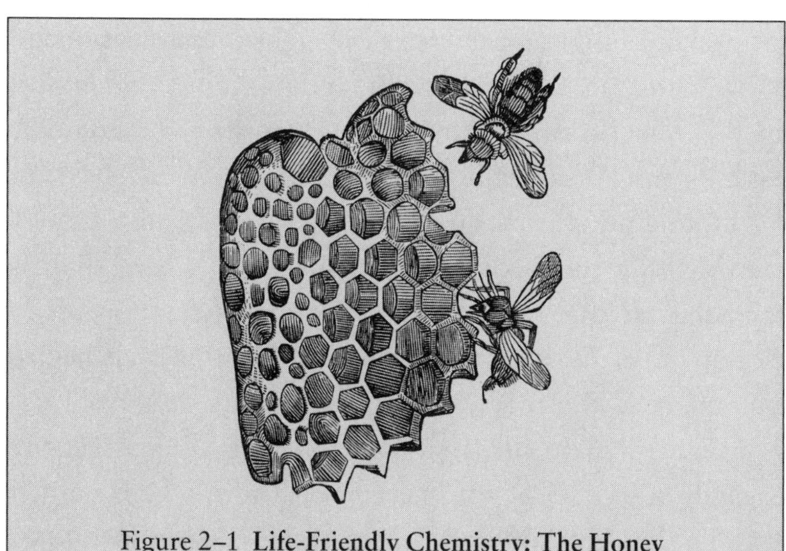

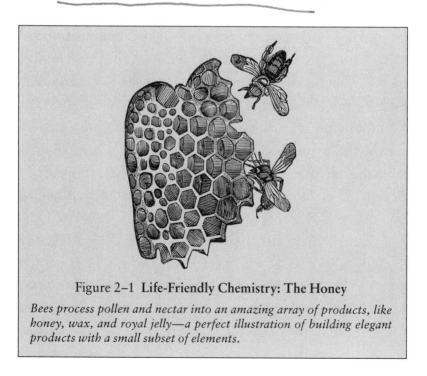

Figure 2–1 **Life-Friendly Chemistry: The Honey**

Bees process pollen and nectar into an amazing array of products, like honey, wax, and royal jelly—a perfect illustration of building elegant products with a small subset of elements.

limits are often a spur to innovation. Instead of focusing energy on creating new components, all of that attention can be focused on creating different, better outcomes. This concept was highlighted in recent years at the LEGO company, where one element of the organization's comeback was shrinking the menu of components that new product designers could work with. The smaller, more limited menu turned out to be the inspiration for much better products.[6] Sometimes the best way to get a terrific out-of-the-box answer is to start with a lot of inside-the-box constraints.

Translation to Investing

Even if you like spiders and French bakeries, this particular principle might seem irrelevant to the investment realm. What constitutes "chemistry" for finance? More importantly, what would "water-based chemistry" or nontoxic assembly and disassembly look like?

I found my way through these challenging questions by starting with the second subprinciple, the "what." This is the principle that talks about using simple components in elegant ways. When I think back to the story that begins this chapter, the magical market-hedging security, I see a product that is clearly a bit misaligned. This security is really a bundle of other securities, all of them market options that link to various performance scenarios. None of the elements in this security is a primary investment transaction or relationship. It's like a financial Twinkie, one synthetic ingredient layered on top of another to form what appears to be a coherent whole.

Now, I have been known to enjoy the occasional Twinkie, but the central question behind life's principles is always "for what purpose?" A Twinkie might provide enjoyment, it might provide caloric intake, but it does not provide true nourishment. So I asked a similar question about the market-hedging security: toward what end? What is the purpose of this creation? What is its **function?**

This proved to be a helpful starting point. The hedging security was designed to provide a sense of comfort, because it would cushion some potential downside in market performance. And it also provided a sense of control, because the purchaser could feel agency, having taken action to protect her capital and perhaps even to grow it. But the key word in those sentences is "sense": a Twinkie provides a sense of indulgence, but it does not provide true nourishment. Likewise, this security provided a sense of comfort and control, but it did not do much to address real underlying risk and uncertainty for the investor.

Thinking through that particular subprinciple of "what" led me back to the other principles of nontoxic production. I was especially struggling with the idea of water-based chemistry: What is the equivalent of water in finance? When we think through the benefits of water as a chemical base, we see that it offers several characteristics: first, it is flexible. Sometimes water is a key catalyst in a chemical reaction, but other times it is a neutral carrier for other elements. And second, water itself is bountiful and nontoxic.

In most environments, it is present before any chemistry takes place and it is there long after, too.

Considering these characteristics, I believe that the "water" in finance is community, connection to the world. When we start and end our investing with community, there is a continuity of chemistry throughout the process, a link that binds investing to activity in society. Sometimes people serve as a vital catalyst in our investing process, and sometimes people are more neutral actors, but they are always present.

In contrast, when we start an investment process with synthetic securities as our ingredients, the only possible output is one that is more and more synthesized, farther and farther from the primary investments that fuel the real economy, that nourish our real communities. People are far away from every stage of this process, and far from its outputs. The problem is that though people are removed from these synthetic creations, we are still impacted by the outcomes, the results that echo back in a powerful way onto the real world and the people in it.

When we want to refocus on "water-based chemistry," then, we need to refocus on the nonsynthetic pieces of finance, the direct transactions and primary relationships that form the authentic core of investing. And what provides the supportive, nontoxic environment in which those primary connections occur? Community of people, links between individuals and all of their various needs, contributions, and endeavors. This is our water.

Those synthetic creations, the Cheez Whiz and Twinkies of finance, are not inherently useless instruments, but we have mistaken them for the real thing, for true nourishment, for solutions to our deepest needs. What's essential are the direct connections, the primary transactions that form the core of investing: the "whole foods of finance." The financial Twinkies need to be around the edges, more rare—not at the center of our investment plates. Moving closer to the primary, unsynthesized forms of investing automatically brings us into closer alignment with life's principles.

Natural Scorecard: Mortgage-Backed Securities

By now, thanks to the financial crisis of 2008, terms like CMO, CDO, and CDO-squared have entered into common use, and everyone seems to understand that many of these creations were ultimately "toxic." The trouble with this line of thinking is that it is just as simplistic as the one that led us into danger in the first place: financial creations are generally not bad or good, but they all have specific characteristics that may solve a certain problem, or may cause a different one. Examining mortgage securities through the lens of nature's nontoxic principles brings a deeper understanding of this nuance.

When I was first assigned to be a housing analyst in the early 1990s, my knowledge of mortgages was mainly drawn from George Bailey's description in *It's a Wonderful Life*. When there's a run on the Bailey Building and Loan, George explains that he doesn't have all of the townspeople's money back in a safe; it's been loaned out to their friends and neighbors, as mortgages on their homes.[7] Turns out, this is not such a bad model to have in mind: in its most essential form, a mortgage is a simple, direct transaction, connected to specific people and specific communities.

Before leaping ahead to the current century's mortgage woes, think of a plain old mortgage on a single-family house. In this transaction, you have a house, a buyer, and a lender. Simple elements, connected directly to one another, with a straightforward mechanism that is easy to unwind. This kind of transaction can bring great benefit: before the mortgage market was developed, you'd have to save up for years and years, or be born into some serious financial luck, to be able to afford a home purchase.

When it comes to disassembly of a conventional mortgage, it's pretty simple. Take apart a traditional mortgage and you are left with those same essential components—a house, a buyer, and a lender—and they can all separate and go on to be reconfigured in different combinations. Importantly, it doesn't matter if these elements separate for happy reasons, like the loan being paid off, or unhappy reasons, like the borrower being unable to repay. Regardless of circumstance, the components are benign.

Compare this sort of simple mortgage against the "life-friendly chemistry" principles:

- **Is there "chemistry in water"?** Are the components all connected in community? A direct transaction, by definition, is tied to specific people and places, so yes.

- **Is the product built selectively, with a small subset of elements?** Yes, a straightforward, old-school loan only needs a lender, borrower, and asset.
- **Does the product break down into benign constituents?** At the end of its life, the loan components can easily separate and go on to other uses, so yes, the breakdown process is benign.

Single, simple mortgages, then, are pretty well aligned with principles of life-friendly creation: they'd earn a grade of A-minus, or perhaps B-plus.

Now, let's look at a more modern version of mortgage finance, the collateralized mortgage obligation (CMO), or its broader financial category, the collateralized debt obligation (CDO). There is a lot of complexity in some of these instruments, but at its heart, all that a CDO does is bundle together loans in order to rearrange the pieces and resell them. In certain circumstances, this kind of arrangement could be very useful: say you are worried about the economy in one geographic area, but you know that a big employer is thriving the next county over. Or say that you've already made a lot of high-risk loans and you want to balance that out with some lower-risk lending. A CMO allows you to mix geographies, borrowers, and loan types in ways that should enable an investor to pick and choose their exposures. This kind of arrangement could also benefit borrowers, since it allows their risk to be mixed together with others, which should generally make their cost to borrow lower.

Though a CMO is more complicated than a simple

mortgage, it can certainly serve some useful purpose. So how is it that this whole category came to be associated with toxicity? Here is a condensed history of what happened to this market in the years heading up to the 2008 financial crisis:

- We saw a rapid increase in the **volume of primary activity**—the aggregate value of those plain old home mortgages in the United States grew from $1.5 trillion in the beginning of 1986 to $11.1 trillion at the end of 2007, an increase of over sevenfold.[8]
- The **nature of primary activity**, those underlying loans, was changing at the same time: in 2006, over 23 percent of all mortgages originated were subprime, compared with levels of under 10 percent before the mid-00s bubble.[9]
- During that same period, the aggregate **level of securitizations was increased.** Mortgage securitizations increased even more than underlying mortgage activity, from $410 billion to $6.4 trillion, an increase of over fifteen-fold (roughly twice as fast as the underlying mortgage activity). Note that this is the total, cumulative level of securitizations, not new issues, and not notional value.
- Mortgage securitizations took on **new and bigger forms** during this period too: at the peak, issuance of new ABS, MBS, and CDO instruments was almost $600 billion in just one quarter (2Q2007).[10]
- Synthetic CDOs provided yet another **extension and abstraction** of activity. These securities are essentially a bet on the performance of other mortgage securities—their value is determined by payment streams on credit default swaps, not from payment streams on loans related

to tangible assets. They are an abstraction of a derivative, related to (but far removed from) actual houses, people, or primary mortgages.[11]

During a short period of time, then, several layers of changes were piled on top of one another: first, primary mortgage activity increased in volume and decreased in quality; second, processing of that primary activity into securitizations increased in both volume and complexity; and third, new synthetic products were created on top of those processed securities. All three layers present problems, and each layer shows less and less alignment with the principles of nontoxic production.

A plain old mortgage was pretty well aligned with the concept of nontoxicity, but now compare the final layer of financial creation, a synthetic CDO, against principles of life-friendly production:

- **Is there "chemistry in water"?** Are the components all connected in community? The whole point of a CDO is to disconnect the components of specific borrowers, assets, and places from one another, in the hopes of reducing risk—and for synthetics this is all the more true. So, the answer is no.
- **Is the product built selectively, with a small subset of elements?** The CDO takes all of the basic elements of individual loans, adds them together, and rearranges them in a purely manufactured way. The synthetic takes this one step further, creating artificial ways to bet on already packaged bundles of securities. No again.

• **Does the product break down into benign constituents?** Because the CDO has rearranged all of the pieces, and then the synthetic has abstracted them even further, these securities are hard to deconstruct. The owner of a CDO effectively owns a little piece of lots and lots of loans, and the owner of a synthetic only owns pieces of credit protection payments, so the breakdown process for any one of these securities is inherently difficult and incomplete.

Synthetic securities began as specialized complements to our basic investing diet, used for unusual circumstances and for particular purposes. In this very specific context, their form might have fit function, even if the composition process was not exactly life-friendly. But we moved these sorts of securities to the center of our investing plates, which pulled a large portion of our financial activity out of alignment with life's principles. By doing so, we needlessly made mortgage financing toxic, no longer conducive to life.

This analysis does not mean there is no role for CDOs or other securitized products in the world, but it does show that there are limits for such products. Once those limits are surpassed, risks are magnified instead of diminished. A rare Twinkie within a mainly kale-and-quinoa diet might be great, but an all-Twinkie approach to nutrition is perilous. The existence of processed securities is not a problem, but their rampant and unnecessary growth facilitated much more investment trauma than could have ever been delivered by organizations like the Bailey Savings and Loan, no matter how many defaults there were in Bedford Falls.

Evolution

Contrary to the mortgage finance example, there is plenty of evidence that less synthesized forms of investing and creation are thriving. For example, there is active discussion in angel investing communities about how to fund "normal growth" companies, those whose business prospects are solid, but where the needs for funding are modest and the complications of selling (and buying) equity are unnecessary. Equity investing in a small start-up company is often a painful process for all concerned, with lots of legal paperwork, expense, and sometimes contentious negotiations between investor and investee. This is a tough way to start a constructive business relationship! For companies where plain vanilla loans are appropriate instead of equity, the basic agreements can often fit on one sheet of paper, and the main terms to negotiate are just time and price—a simple set of parameters.

Simpler forms of consumer banking also seem to be seeing a revival. One of the most popular programs of Green America in recent years is their "Break Up with Your Mega-Bank" guide, which helps individuals seek out local banks and credit unions that might serve their needs better than a large financial institution.[12] In the United States, credit union assets crossed the $1 trillion mark in 2012, and the industry reported record earnings.[13] After several waves of bank consolidation throughout the 1990s and 2000s, I found that my account had migrated from a small local bank to a big national one, without my ever deciding to make that switch. Ultimately, I wanted and needed the service of a smaller institution, and so I switched back to a group with more direct and personal customer connections—more aligned with life-friendly principles.

Similarly, platforms like Kickstarter and Kiva allow for direct links between investors, supporters, inventors, and small business owners. Different forms of crowd funding, like Mosaic Energy, offer similar potential, though there are still lots of regulatory complexities to be sorted out. In these cases, the platforms also put the decision of **how to invest** back in the hands of the actual investor: some enable support in the form of gifts, some in the form of loans, some in the form of product purchase. The forms of support are simpler, which means you don't need lots of layers of processing between you and your investment.

Pathway to Practice

How can we avoid the "Twinkie portfolio"? As with our other life's principles, this one offers some clear pathways to progress: instead of just asking about mechanics of an investment or its clever design, begin by asking **"to what end?"** If the proposition is merely clever, but not serving a vital need, move on. If it *is* serving that vital need, then ask how. Can you trace its connection to real products, real people, real communities? Can you identify the simple elements that are elegantly assembled to make it? Can you look ahead and envision a benign, straightforward disassembly process or sale?

Once this set of principles becomes engrained in our thinking, we can extend our incorporation of them to other layers of investing. If you are comfortable that a fund's construction aligns with life-friendly chemistry, what about all of its subcomponents? What about its managers? What about their sales processes or the infrastructure of their supporting operations?

I don't mean to keep harping on Cheez Whiz, but the analogy is a great one. Once we realize we might want more cheese than cheez in our diet (or better yet, less cheez and more carrots), we naturally start asking, what about the bread? What about the person making the sandwich? What about the city that surrounds the sandwich stand?

As we examine each layer, we get closer and closer to deeper, more complete alignment.

We live in a society that values technology, innovation, and creativity. Importantly, this "life-friendly chemistry" concept does not need to be at odds with those values. Instead, it reorients them, demanding even more elegant, effective solutions.

In an investment context, this means that if we've been solving a problem with a synthetic solution, we demand an organic one, one that is simpler and yet just as effective. Or better yet, we reexamine the problem to see if it can be solved another way—perhaps in a way that requires an elegant, personal, artisanal approach rather than a product that was designed for ease of manufacture and infinite scalability. This might seem harder and less efficient than an "off the shelf" solution, of course—but were you here in 2008 and 2009? Is it really harder than that? What was the price of that efficiency?

If we need yield, we might find a few simple stocks or bonds that serve that purpose, rather than a complicated CDO-type product. Or we may find a local business that needs a loan, where we understand the risks and want to support their mission. Or we may ultimately question, why do I need that yield in the first place? Is it enabling something in my life that I truly value, or have I just been told I need it so often that I've forgotten to ask why?

Rather than asking, "Can you make me a purple Twinkie?" we are asking, "Can you make me a cream-filled, curiously shaped cake without all of these chemicals?" Or maybe even, "Can you make me a salad that is so good I forget I about the cake?" Now *that* is a worthy challenge!

Sowing Seeds of Nontoxic Investing

Here are some simple ideas that help to start us along the "life-friendly" path:

- **Consider the core purpose** of any synthetic investment: Is it performing a function that you really need? Is it performing that function well?
- **Simplify.** If you are tempted to buy a security that claims to manage S&P risk, perhaps that means you really just want less exposure to stocks in the first place. There are usually simpler ways to achieve any given purpose than buying a highly processed investment product.
- **Invest with the goal of elegant simplicity,** not needless complication. Aim for a few investments that are simple,

suitable, and easily disassembled, rather than a Twinkie portfolio.

By aiming for simple, "organic" forms of investing, we can avoid some of the risks of toxicity that are inherent in overly processed products. We can eliminate needless synthetic creations and come closer to investing in a connected, integrated way.

We can move from processed complexity to elegant simplicity.

We can shift from synthetic to organic.

Transformation 3

From Maximized to Optimized

"What's with the share count?" my colleague glanced up at me, eyebrows raised skeptically as he looked at my freshly constructed spreadsheet.

"Ummmm…" I frowned at the paper, willing it to offer up insight. Alas, it was silent.

"Okay," he sighed. "This company is growing, right?"

"Right!"

"It says here they are opening fifty more stores next year, right?"

"Right!"

"And it costs about two million dollars to open each store, right?"

"Right!"

"So how are they gonna pay for that?"

"Ohhhhh."

"Exactly. They'll need more funding. So fix the share count and then let's talk."

This was the exchange between me, a brand-new equity analyst looking at her first retail company, and one of my colleagues who managed a large growth-oriented mutual fund. (Yes, the details have been changed to be slightly more polite than the exchange that actually occurred). Luckily, because of this sort of conversation, I learned early on that in order for any endeavor to grow, some form of additional resource is required (in this case, issuing more stock, so that the company had more cash, so that it could pay for the new stores). This is a notion that is completely transparent when we consider growth of a seedling, or a baby—they obviously can't grow without nutrients. But when it comes to business and finance, sometimes we like to pretend that we can conjure growth out of thin air, with no resources required beyond our own imaginations.

Growth is not just a wish and a prayer, nor a goal unto itself. To be effective, growth needs to be integrated with development.

Nature's Principle: Integrate Development with Growth

Growth is a deeply embedded assumption in many human endeavors. To balance out this simplistic frame of mind we have nature's principle, **integrate development with growth.** The most important element is that this is an "and" statement: growth and development need to occur hand in hand, not one separate from the other. Think of a sunflower, where the stem can grow several feet in just a couple of weeks. What is unseen, but completely necessary, is the root structure of the sunflower, which is growing with just as much fervor down and across the soil, to anchor that stem. And still, we can see examples every year at the end of the season where a giant, seed-laden head just proves too much for the infrastructure of the plant, and the whole sunflower topples over, uprooted by its own top-heavy weight. Who wants to be that sunflower? A truly balanced "and" embedded within "development and growth" prevents a brilliant growth spurt from an eventual crash.

The subprinciples of **integrate development with growth** are:

- Combine modular and nested components.
- Build from the bottom up.
- Self-organize.

The subprinciples of development and growth give important answers to the question of "how." We could easily envision a plan that integrates development and growth in a highly engineered way, but the first subprinciple emphasizes, **combine modular and nested components.** The idea is not merely to grow larger, but to grow in ways that are repeatable and that fit together as an organism grows. Consider an octopus—it does not have one huge mega-arm or eight arms with completely different designs (though that might make for a cool cartoon character). An octopus has smaller suckers that grow to larger suckers, and they're aligned in regular patterns along each of its limbs, allowing it to grow in a way that is both efficient and effective. In fact, even within each sucker an octopus has modular components: there are three sorts of muscles that all work together to make the sucker function.[1] This is what we mean by **modular and nested** components.

When growth is approached in that modular way, it is easier to envision a system that is **built from the bottom up.** A mangrove island can become a robust structure, but not through fancy preplanned blueprints or top-down engineering. A single seed sprouts and its roots begin to slow the water around it, which helps to settle more sand and more seeds nearby. Then organisms begin to live among the roots and add organic matter until the sand becomes soil. This system is **built from the bottom up**, and the growth is internally generated; though systems take on energy from the outside, the actual *creation* happens from the bottom up, from within. Of course there is value to blueprints and planning, but there is also value to systems that allow for self-organizing growth. It need not be one or the other.

The classic example of a **self organized** system is an ant colony, where the function of the whole is optimized through the actions of individual members. For example, some individual ants have more sensitivity to hunger, and they are the first to leave the nest in search of food. If the food is more broadly needed within the colony, other gatherers will soon follow the first ones out to search for nourishment. Communication within the system is optimized as well, with scouts leaving positive pheromone trails toward the good food sources and negative trails when their searches have not borne fruit.[2] There is no ant commander in chief, no strategic plan for the colony sitting on a little underground shelf: all of these individual activities, along with appropriate feedback loops, enable an optimized total system.

This principle seems easy to apply on the surface. Of course growth requires development alongside it, focus on the supporting structures that allow expansion to be solid and sustained. But delving into the subprinciples, we find some more intriguing ideas:

First, these principles encourage us to move from a linear growth/nongrowth mind-set to a more **integrated point of view.** Instead of choosing to invest in development *or* growth, they compel us to invest in *both.* The first questions for investors should not be "How fast is this investment growing?" but rather, "*Why* is it growing?" and "*How* is it growing?" In fact, in many situations the most important topic to explore is whether an endeavor can shrink in an elegant, nondisruptive way, returning resources to the environment when conditions warrant it.

The second embedded concept is a shift from **top-down controls to bottom-up activity.** At first this idea might seem to be just the opposite of the managerial approach taken in many of our traditional (and successful) organizations, where complex business planning exercises and intricate monitoring systems seem prevalent. But a closer examination of this principle shows that the idea is "to create conditions that allow components of a system to work toward an enriched system," and to result in a whole that is more than the sum of the parts.

I confess that my first reaction to this particular idea was to tick off a list of all of the reasons for a company to refuse to model itself after an ant colony. Aren't we different? Aren't we special? Aren't we more sophisticated? Upon further reflection, I realized that the very best groups I've been associated with actually embrace this notion of self-organization, though few label it as such.

For example, for a number of years, I led one of the largest investment research groups in the world—an endeavor that was both complex and complicated, to say the least. Thankfully, this role did not entail running around to each analyst telling him what to do that day—and if it had, the results would have been disastrous for all concerned. Instead, the leadership of our group tried to set clear objectives, the "what," and perhaps more importantly, clear guidelines for "how," in terms of responsibility, collaboration, and integrity. Then it was up to each member of our team to figure out how her own work could best contribute to the whole. Once in the early years of my career a competitor referred to our research team as "the Borg," because we seemed to have one giant collective mind. I don't think he meant it as a compliment, but I thought it was kind of cool (minus the intergalactic warfare, that is). Not too different from a beehive, a mycelial network, or, yes, a termite colony.

In order for that sort of bottom-up organization to be effective, these principles also emphasize the concept of **simple rules** to govern each part of the system and to guide the development and growth of the whole. Unfortunately, within finance, this crucial element seems to be at odds with an ever more complicated maze of regulatory, tax, and market-related complexity that grows more and more weighty every year. When I think of simple rules, I recall the first compliance agreement I ever signed as an employee of a big financial firm. It was a few pages long, presented with great (and appropriate) solemnity, and said, in essence, "I promise not to do anything that goes against the interests of our own shareholders." Fast-forward twenty years, and compliance agreements in financial firms look like phone books: page after page of byzantine "what if" scenarios, backed up by floors full of lawyers who try to monitor activity via endless data reports. There are some good reasons why all that complication has developed, but the net result is often to make participants feel less power and responsibility, not more. The slim documents of old essentially said, "We trust you—sign this so we are officially aligned," while the current mega-documents seem to say, "We don't trust you, and you could never really comprehend everything that's in here—sign this so we can punish you later."

When we add these ideas about integrated growth and development together, we do not see a recipe for the common "command-and-control" models seen in some of our largest organizations, nor do we see a detailed up-front blueprint process like those employed in some of our largest structural creations. However, alignment with this set of life's principles does not mean that our human constructions should go without planning or guidance. Instead, these principles remind us of the true function of planning, leadership, and management: planning and leadership are best seen as the process of setting those simple rules that govern a system. Management—whether of an organization or an investment portfolio—is best seen as setting in place appropriate feedback loops. Those loops can incorporate new information and assess needs for new or different resources, thus ensuring that growth *and* development are both supported.

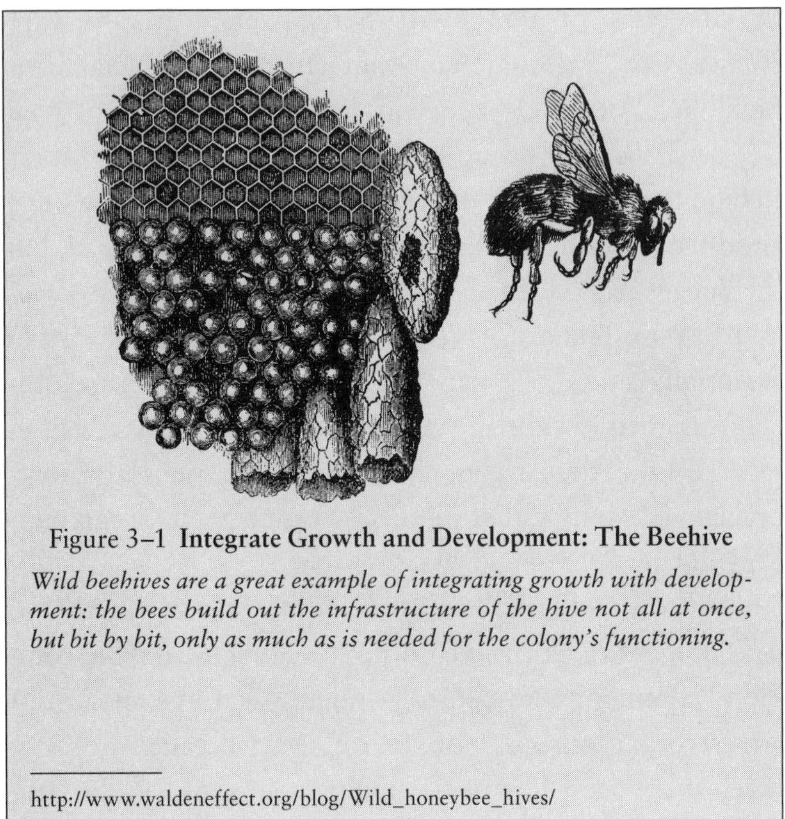

Figure 3–1 **Integrate Growth and Development: The Beehive**

Wild beehives are a great example of integrating growth with development: the bees build out the infrastructure of the hive not all at once, but bit by bit, only as much as is needed for the colony's functioning.

---

http://www.waldeneffect.org/blog/Wild_honeybee_hives/

Translation to Investing

Before moving to specific financial examples, it is important to stop to consider the fundamental idea of **growth** as it relates to investing. The assumption that underpins almost all of our products, processes, and procedures is not just that growth is good, but that it is required, our central objective. And if growth is good, more growth must be better. Fast growth and big growth must be best of all.

Sometimes this thirst for growth translates to a passion for business concepts like "scalability." But nature does not scale, at least not to an infinite degree. Nature replicates. Nature develops. Unlimited growth in investing is thought to be nirvana, but unchecked growth in nature is, quite literally, disease. It's cancer.

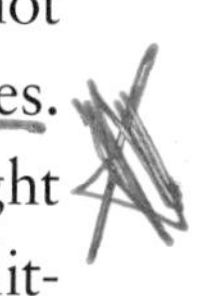

This mismatch between growth in nature and growth in finance is worth serious consideration. And again, it circles around to the core concepts of **context and connection.** As we've already discovered, it's been increasingly common to disconnect financial activity from reality, and yet, at the end of the day, there are still physical limits to growth. These limits are increasingly obvious on a planetary level, but it's easier to think of a simple natural example like a pumpkin. If you want to eat the pumpkin, you aim for the smallest, sweetest varieties: trust me, growing them bigger just makes for stringy, watery pumpkin pies. But if you want to win the pumpkin-boat contest in Damariscotta, Maine, you want the biggest, strongest, lightest vegetable possible. Different contexts, different approaches. And yet when it comes to investing, usually we settle for feeble distinctions by referencing financial risk–return trade-offs, ignoring all of the other vital dimensions of growth, measurement, and success.

Indeed, it is rare for an investment policy statement to *not* include the word "growth." Even in our philanthropic organizations, it is unusual to see a plan for shrinking assets over time, though the entire premise of a charitable foundation's existence is to give money away. Of course, one reason that many of us invest is (at least in part—and often in large part) to grow our own resources. But it is helpful to pause to return to the central question of biomimicry, the central question of life: "**Toward what end?** What is the purpose?" Related to this is the question we usually skip, "Growth of what?" Without thinking, we usually give our growth targets in dollars or percentage points, but there are many other dimensions to consider. We could aim for growth of community, or growth of supportive infrastructure, or growth of tangible asset values, or growth of personal fulfillment. At the very least, we could root for growth of long-term economic value rather than growth in reported earnings per share.

After the what, we need to consider **why.** Why do we want growth, whether it's of dollars or apple trees or joy? Is it to fuel consumption? Is it to build up security for uncertain times? It is to provide for future generations? Is it simply to "win"? These could all be legitimate reasons under certain circumstances, but they are *different* reasons, and they point to different pathways to guide us from here to there. Perhaps most importantly, they also point to different sorts of development that might be needed along the way.

Finally, we need to ask not just how much, but **how?** Almost every endeavor offers the chance to maximize short-term growth in an inefficient, wasteful manner. But every good businessperson recognizes that this approach is just hurting his own enterprise; a much more interesting question is, can growth be achieved in a way that is not just sustainable, but regenerative? This is perhaps the biggest question for the world economies, too: Can we fuel healthy standards of living for all, in a way that uses fewer physical resources, instead of more?

A mechanized, one-size-fits-all approach to growth maximization might be efficient, but it is decidedly not effective. What we need is growth combined with development—optimized, not maximized. Multi-dimensional growth, not just "bigger."

Natural Scorecard: High-Frequency Trading

High-frequency trading provides a fascinating case study for the principles of growth and development. This segment of finance, and its acronym, "HFT," is beginning to be spoken of with the same ominous overtones as CDOs, as the activity of these firms has been blamed for several "flash crash" events as well as for boosting overall market volatility. In light of these events, to simply declare that high-frequency trading is "bad" might feel satisfying, but it is not an intellectually rigorous statement. And all of us would recognize that some level of market making, whether in stocks or potatoes or time exchange, is part of a healthy, ongoing economic ecosystem. Examining high-frequency trading through the lens of "integrate growth and development" provides a more nuanced understanding.

First, a clear definition is in order: high-frequency trading is not the same as market making, and it is not the same as "the" market. At its core, a high-frequency trading firm does the same thing that dozens of others do: it matches buy and sell orders on securities, in this case via electronic trading platforms. And, as the name implies, it does so very, very fast. HFTs often complete transactions in milliseconds or even microseconds. (A microsecond is a millionth of a second; it takes several hundred milliseconds—three hundred thousand microseconds—to blink your eye.) In addition to acting as traders for others, many HFT firms also trade for themselves, using quantitative trading algorithms for their own purposes.

I call this the "spin class" approach to trading: if you want a really efficient workout, when the perky instructor at the front yells, "Faster!" you obey, pedaling until your legs are just a blur, they are moving so fast. Likewise, when markets seemed to require more liquidity, participants naturally called out, "Faster!" and the high-frequency trading firms obliged, cranking up volumes and speed until transactions were just a blur, moving so fast that they are literally unmatchable by human eyes, let alone human brains and human judgment.

But the thing about spin class is, it ends. We are not meant to stay at peak activity levels forever, and once a workout is over, there is always time to recover. Again, this reflects a cycle of integrated development and growth. With the market, though, spin class has become eternal. Policies and practices that made sense in times of extreme duress were codified so that they became the norm—a permanent peak workout in trading volumes. This constant focus on speed and growth might be a clever mechanical trick, but it is not a characteristic of a healthy ecosystem.

Yet when it comes to growth, few sectors of finance can

compare with the record growth of HFT in the mid-2000s. In 2005, this activity represented about 21 percent of total market volume, but by 2009, this figure was a whopping 61 percent. Overall market volume had also grown significantly during this period, from about four billion shares of U.S. stocks traded daily to just under ten billion, but if you look closely at those numbers you'll see that most of that growth (about 90 percent) was accounted for by the growth in HFT.[3] If we picture the market as a tree, and all of the different trading firms as branches, the HFT branches grew all out of proportion to the rest of the tree during this period. We've all seen weird, lopsided growth spurts like this in nature, and it's easy to see how they are resolved: either the other parts of the tree have to develop to catch up with the runaway limbs, or eventually, something will break and crash to the ground. The whole tree could even be destroyed.

When we compare the basic activity of high-frequency trading against the "integrate growth and development" principles, here's what we find:

- **Does HFT combine modular and nested components in its construction?** Each trade is an individual action, and each piece of a trading algorithm is also discrete. When these pieces are nested together, that's when the whole firm and whole algorithmic approach are revealed. So, there is some evidence of using modular and nested components.
- **Does HFT build from the bottom up?** These firms do not begin by examining the entire market and then carving off slices where they'll participate. Each trade, each

security, each exchange presents individual opportunities, and these aggregate to form overall activity. So, there is some evidence of building from the bottom up.

• **Does HFT demonstrate self-organizing principles?** The concept behind a trading algorithm is to create simple rules to guide activity (of course, the simple rules are wrapped in elegant, perhaps complicated, code). And the business concept behind most HFTs is that gathering up tiny profits over and over again creates good business results. In theory, at least, this idea is not so far from life's principle of self-organization.

The answer to all of these questions is "sort of." HFT in and of itself is not in clear alignment with the natural principles of growth and development, but it is not obviously misaligned either. A grade of C, maybe C-plus.

But now let's consider a more systemic view of high-frequency trading, along with a less benign backdrop: the "flash crash" of 2010. On May 6, 2010, the Dow plunged over 9 percent in midafternoon, only to recover most of that ground by the close of the day. There have been several smaller, similar events since then, but the 2010 example is the most vivid and the most studied to date.

By 2010, high frequency trading was over half of market volume, so naturally, when the flash crash was analyzed, activity of these firms was a crucial piece of the analysis. The video depictions of trading during the flash crash are especially eerie: they show order routing between the major trading firms, with each firm a node at the edge of a big circle.[4] At first the flow looks just like a bunch of bees flying between nectar sources and beehives, or balls on a playground: dots flying regularly to and from each major node. And then, suddenly, the flow stops. Every once in a while a signal pulses out from one of the hubs into space, but it's met with silence. No response. When I watch these trade-flow images, I am still oddly shaken. In many market crises, trading *values* fall dramatically, but trading *volume* is still very active. Watching these depictions, where activity just stops altogether, is like watching a living organism die.

Explanations for the flash crash are long, multilayered, and still subject to some dispute, but consider these facts:

- The official SEC explanation of the flash crash centers on a single order to sell futures contracts with a value of just over $4 billion. The sell order caused pressure not just on the contracts in question, but on the stocks related to those contracts, and the ripple effects of the resulting volatility caused some traders to step back, while other automated programs continued unchecked.[5]
- According to the New York Stock Exchange, part of the problem was a mismatch where systems at the NYSE are meant to automatically *slow* trading during extremely volatile times, whereas the systems at some HFT firms are, if anything, designed to speed up as volatility increases.[6]
- As part of the investigation process in 2010, the Commodities Futures Trading Commission (CTFC), the equivalent of the SEC for commodities trading, created a technology

advisory committee of quantitative traders and other technological experts. An advisory committee like this had not existed for five years—the same five years when HFT was growing from 20 percent to 60 percent of trading volume.[7]

• One critique of the SEC investigation is that the time increments it used for analysis are too long (the report accounts for second-by-second trading activity on that day). Alternate analytical views favor timing measures of just twenty-five milliseconds for their analysis. It is hard for our analysis to match the pace of trading, even in retrospect, when we have all the time in the world to calculate and consider.

Our goal here is not to decipher or debate the exact causes of the flash crash, but rather to highlight some clear systemic mismatches, areas where growth was decidedly *not* aligned with development. Though our assessment of HFT as a single component in the system showed some potential for alignment with life's principles, this inquiry into the broader trading landscape clearly shows a system that contains seriously misaligned elements. The growth in high-frequency trading was decidedly *not* supported by commensurate development in all of the structures needed for healthy function. There was *not* growth in the rest of the trading market alongside the growth in HFT. There was *not* development of oversight or technical expertise in other parts of the system to appropriately incorporate the rise of HFT. There was *not* progress in related systems like the NYSE's so that their functions aligned with (or complemented) those of high-frequency firms.

Comparing the overgrown version of HFT systems with

the principles of "integrate growth with development," we find considerably less alignment than before:

- **Does HFT combine modular and nested components in its construction?** Though each organization, each process, and even each trade might be shown to be in partial alignment with these principles, each of them also demonstrates some areas of misalignment. And in this case, when all those pieces of the system are assembled and under duress, the cracks are magnified and the entire system is *less* aligned than its parts.
- **Does HFT build from the bottom up?** There was no way for the structures, systems, processes, or regulations embedded in the individual organisms (other parts of the system) to evolve fast enough to match the growth of high-frequency trading.
- **Does HFT demonstrate self-organizing principles?** The feedback loops were weak and often did not extend beyond the walls of any single participant in the system. Connections between participants extended far beyond counterparties for any given trade, and yet these links were underestimated.

Even the SEC concluded, "May 6 was also an important reminder of the interconnectedness of our derivatives and securities markets."[8] A system lacking in understanding of its multilayered connections, lacking in feedback loops that incorporate them effectively, lacking in mechanisms that allow for rapid evolution . . . this is a system incapable of integrating development with growth.

Evolution

Growth discussions are often most feverish when we discuss early-stage ventures, and for good reason: often, without rapid growth, these fragile ventures fail. Within this entrepreneurial arena, there are several hopeful developments.

First, the notion of "fail fast" has taken hold in many new ventures. This idea recognizes the inherent fragility of any new endeavor, and instead of denying that fragility, encourages participants to embrace it, planning for small experiments, quick assessments, and, if need be, graceful endings. The focus is not exactly on failure, but on cultivating an ability to quickly test, assess, and adapt. Building this concept of modular testing and designing with appropriate feedback loops from the very beginning of an enterprise is a fundamentally different starting point from the twentieth-century "deep research, big bet" approach, which was in part necessitated by much more capital-intensive businesses. If you failed fast back then, you often did not have the resources to adapt and try again.

Second, more attention has been paid to the "development" part of development and growth in recent years: dozens of incubators and mentor programs are available for entrepreneurs now, whether they are writing new software in a loft or training rural health-care workers half a world away. The communities that are arising among these incubators, innovation corridors, and entrepreneurial hubs are adding to the diversity, vibrancy, and strength of the overall system. Additionally, there is more attention paid to the fundamental capital intensity of early-stage business models, which often relates to the ongoing resource-intensity of those same businesses. Growing a software business has a fundamentally different set of needs than growing a lumber business, and those differences are becoming better understood by entrepreneurs, managers, customers, and investors.

Most importantly, our definitions of growth and growth's purpose have begun to expand. Alternate, more multidimensional views of prosperity are extending far beyond the narrowness of standard measures like gross domestic product. Measures like the Social Progress Index and gross national happiness are being discussed in the halls of Davos and Harvard Business School,[9] and are beginning to address the shortcomings made famous by Robert Kennedy in his 1968 speech:

> ...gross national product counts air pollution and cigarette advertising, and ambulances to clear our highways of carnage. It counts special locks for our doors and the jails for the people who break them. It counts the destruction of the redwood and the loss of our natural wonder in chaotic sprawl. It counts napalm and counts nuclear warheads and armored cars for the police to fight the riots in our cities. It counts Whitman's rifle and Speck's knife, and the television programs which glorify violence in order to sell toys to our children. Yet the gross national product does not allow for the health of our children, the quality of their education or the joy of their play. It does not include the beauty of

> our poetry or the strength of our marriages, the intelligence of our public debate or the integrity of our public officials. It measures neither our wit nor our courage, neither our wisdom nor our learning, neither our compassion nor our devotion to our country, it measures everything in short, except that which makes life worthwhile. And it can tell us everything about America except why we are proud that we are Americans.[10]

As our definitions expand, they can more accurately reflect true cost and true profit, allowing us to make more thoughtful, complete investment decisions, both as individuals and as societies.

Along with the rapid growth in social entrepreneurs, we are seeing a generation of new businesspeople for whom "double bottom line" and "triple bottom line" are needless fabrications. These servant-leaders take an integrated view from the very beginning, considering growth of impact, growth of scale, and growth of finances in an intertwined, multifaceted way.

Many of these new entrepreneurs follow in the footsteps of predecessors like Judy Wicks, owner of the White Dog Café in Philadelphia. Given the huge success of the café, Judy was constantly urged to grow her business through franchising or other physical duplications. But she chose otherwise:

> Instead of making business decisions to maximize profits, I made decisions to maximize relationships. And in the long run, I believe this was also the reason for our financial sustainability. I had come to realize that we

> could measure our success in other ways than growing physically. We could grow by increasing our knowledge, expanding our consciousness, deepening our relationships, developing our creativity, building community, and enhancing our natural environment. All this while also increasing our own happiness and well-being, and having more fun.[11]

This sort of multidimensional growth reflects a more resilient approach, with multilayered, powerful benefits. And importantly, it provides an example of growth that does not rely on constantly increasing use of natural resources. Just the opposite, it helps to regenerate community ecosystems and natural ecosystems alike.

This breadth of definitions is also echoed in the B-corp (benefit corporation) movement, where businesses explicitly embrace goals that go beyond their financial statements, reminding us of the many forms of impact that our enterprises can have. The B-corp "Declaration of Interdependence" reminds us that all of our endeavors have multidimensional elements that link to a broader social web, and that acknowledging this connection is the first step toward healthy, long-term development. B corps "compete not just to be the best *in* the world, but to be the best *for* the world."[12]

Pathway to Practice

How can we avoid financial activity that is the equivalent of a never-ending spin class? The life's principle "integrate growth with development" offers some clear pathways.

Instead of assuming that growth and speed are inherently good, we can pause to question the purpose and nature of those characteristics. Do we need growth in sheer size, or in complexity, or in redundancy? Do we need greater speed, or the ability to modulate speed as conditions change? Some of the initial growth in HFT brought benefits to overall market liquidity, at a time when that liquidity was a vital "nutrient" for the market and in short supply. But just as farmers adjust techniques to suit varied soil and weather conditions, we need to continually re-ask the fundamental question, what is needed here? What is needed now? Maybe the answer is "more," but the obvious follow-on question is "More *what?*" And why?

Once we see growth and development as intertwined concepts, it's impossible to separate them. The extension of these twin ideas to other sorts of investing is almost unavoidable: If we are looking at a stock, how (and why) is the company planning to grow? Have they thought through all of their "nutrients" and planned for them as carefully as they are planning for financial results? Do conditions warrant a plan for elegant ways to shrink and return nutrients to the broader system, instead of pushing for resource-intensive ways to grow? If we are looking at municipal bonds, they quickly become much more interesting and multifaceted than a simple scan of yields to maturity. What is happening in the municipality? Is there a healthy mix of employers, citizens, infrastructure? Is the bond based on one giant mega-development, without other community supports around it?

As we extend the application of this growth and development principle, we can move from a mind-set of "either/or" to one of "and," from unidimensional to multidimensional.

Sowing Seeds of Integrated Growth and Development

Here are some fundamental considerations to help us move toward balanced, integrated growth and development:

- **Reexamine the fundamental purpose** of growth. Growth in what? In what way? Over what time period? With what characteristics? Toward what purpose? Try to avoid the automatic "more is better" presumption.
- **Balance investments in growth with investments in development.** This is helpful on a micro level, as we look at individual investment decisions, and on a macro level, as we consider our overarching purpose in investing. Constantly ask, where do we need to add resources to support the type of growth that we seek?
- **Accept that spin class is meant to end.** When we find ourselves in investment discussions where the premise is never-ending, effortless growth, recognize that that premise is fiction—unsustainable, unhealthy, or both. How can we develop systems that slow, stop growing, or shrink in elegant

ways? At the very least, how can we focus on endeavors that can grow output or outcomes in ways that do not grow in physical resource intensity at the same time?

We can invest in multiple dimensions simultaneously, redeploying current resources to build up supports for the future, instead of harvesting everything in sight for current use.

We can consider growth and development more broadly and fully.

We can plan for graceful shrinking, conserving and recycling resources for other times and other endeavors.

We can move from a framework of maximization to one of optimization.

Transformation 4

From Disconnected to Reconnected

Over the past twenty years, I've had the joy of traveling to more than twenty countries with Habitat for Humanity, offering manual labor to assist local homeowners as they constructed their houses. On one of my early trips to Africa, the leader of the local Habitat group showed us the storeroom, which was just a small shed with tools and a few bags of cement. I was confused—where were all the other building materials? Having been an analyst covering the home-building industry in the United States, I was used to seeing big stockpiles of materials near any building site.

Soon enough, I realized where the materials were: they were all around us. In the coming days, we took an oxcart down to the riverbank to shovel sand, which we then sifted by hand before mixing into mortar. We walked to the pump down the road to gather water in big, ten-gallon containers, many times each day. We dug clay from the very spot where the house was going to be located, shaping it into bricks for the walls. We went out to the woods to cut lumber for the roof framing. Aside from those bags of cement, a handful of nails, and galvanized metal sheets for the roof, the materials were all hyperlocal.

Even more importantly, the entire community was involved in the building process. Extended family, friends, and neighbors all helped on the jobsite. Some provided food and shelter for visitors. Others provided moral support, stopping by to cheer on the work and to comment on progress. The new house was not just situated within the community; its very construction was a community activity—completely locally attuned. A community investment.

Nature's Principle: Be Locally Attuned and Responsive

Sometimes I think the challenges of our current financial systems can be traced to the early days of space exploration, or perhaps the original *Star Trek* series. These modern-day versions of "the final frontier" reinvigorated our zest for stretching and exploring, a concept that has captivated humans for centuries. They exemplified a noble form of exploration, worthy of serious dedication, resources, and sacrifice. They reminded an entire society of the joy of discovery, of stretching physical boundaries in addition to intellectual boundaries and technological boundaries.

In many ways, however, our notion of exploration is curiously limited. We often tend to take a tourist's view, focusing on what we can bring back from our travels, whether that be greater insights, beautiful photos, goofy T-shirts, new language skills, or moon rocks. In a business and investment context, there is a similar limitation:

we often focus on what can be transacted across great distances, rather than on what can be connected. With the click of a button I can buy stocks in Hong Kong, order clothes from London, or book a plane ticket to India, though none of those activities mean that I've got any real relationships in those places. Our essential notion of going afar seems inextricably linked to exchange and to our own return, rather than creating ongoing connection.

After a prolonged, intense period of globalization, the idea of being "locally attuned" might sound quaint—something you do on the weekends at the farmers' market, before stocking up at Target, or jetting off to Monday's business meeting three thousand miles away. However, the natural principles of being locally attuned are not quaint, and they are not focused on a simple notion of physical proximity; they encompass a more complete concept of **life in context.**

The subprinciples of **"be locally attuned and responsive"** are:

- Use readily available materials and energy.
- Cultivate cooperative relationships.
- Leverage cyclic processes.
- Use feedback loops.

Much like the Habitat houses I've seen around the world, bird nests are great examples of the first subprinciple of life in context: use **readily available materials and energy.** Every backyard explorer has found bird nests made of shredded newspaper, bits of string, and other handy materials, in addition to grasses and twigs. Another illustration is the sea urchin, which can regenerate its spines by precipitating calcite that is already present in the ocean.[1] As part of living in context, natural organisms constantly build with abundant, accessible materials and energy, making use of what's available in the local context. Sometimes this subprinciple is interpreted as the "free stuff" principle—using whatever is there—but that's not quite accurate. We see nature using freely *available* materials, but they aren't literally free. When a bird is collecting twigs or fluff for her nest, there is a big expense of energy involved, as well as some level of risk. Those are costly elements in bird land, anything but free.

Being locally attuned is not limited to materials; it also applies to local relationships. Nature offers plenty of examples to illustrate the second subprinciple, **cultivate cooperative relationships**. Think of the combination of clownfish and certain sorts of sea anemones. The anemone has stinging tentacles, and this keeps most other organisms away. But the clownfish has a protective mucus coating, so it can live with the anemone, sheltered by those same tentacles. In turn, the clownfish cleans food debris around the anemone and scares away the anemone's main predator, the butterfly fish. New research also shows that the quick motions of the clownfish bring extra oxygen to the anemone at nighttime, when oxygen levels are otherwise low.[2] It's easy to humanize or romanticize these kinds of relationships, as many an animated movie has shown us. However, these cooperative connections work not because of sentiment, but because the exchange provides real value for both parties.

Living in context also involves being in sync with local

cycles, and capitalizing on those cycles to support life. This third subprinciple, **leverage cyclic processes,** can be observed in the amazing Namib beetle, which thrives in the desert. The beetle takes advantage of the fog that sweeps over the sand dunes at dawn (a cyclic process). When the fog comes, the beetle raises its shell up so that the water condenses on the upturned surface. The shell has bumps that attract water at the tips and channels that then guide the droplets right into the beetle's mouth.[3]

Finally, it's important to note that living in context is inherently a dynamic process. To continue to thrive over time, it's vital to **use feedback loops and information flows.** For example, you might have seen those cute meerkats on television in recent years. Well, in addition to being fascinating reality stars, the meerkats are tremendous users of feedback loops. These animals eat a lot of scorpions, and as you might imagine, that's a tricky proposition. Adult meerkats have some immunity to scorpion venom, but if you're a young meerkat, it's still important that you learn how to eat a scorpion without being stung. The adults are great teachers here: first they bring the little meerkats dead scorpions for dinner with the tails bitten off, then they bring live scorpions without tails, then eventually the full live scorpions, stingers and all.[4] The little meerkats learn through this iterative instruction, with all of the feedback loops the lessons provide.

There are three crucial components to effective feedback loops. First you need the signal—the information flow. Second, you need a receptor—the information needs to be received in an accurate and useable form. And finally, you need an appropriate response—not just any reaction, but an *appropriate* one. All three of these components need to align, as they do for the young meerkats.

When we translate the natural principles of being locally attuned to a social context, there are a few vital themes to consider. First is the importance of **context**. These principles talk about fitting in to our local environments, but more than that, they require connecting and integrating with those local systems. To thrive in any context we need local inputs, local relationships, and local feedback loops. Anyone who's worked or lived in a group setting can easily see these layers: think of the high school cafeteria. It's not too hard to fit in on a basic level, to find a spot in the lunchroom where you are nourished and don't disrupt the rest of the system. But to find your favorite items in the cafeteria line, to have a table of friends to join, to change plans for tomorrow based on conversations and new offerings from the lunch ladies—that is real integration, life in context.

The second major theme is one of **cooperation and connection**. To be locally attuned means to be locally connected, and those relationships all require some level of cooperation. Sometimes it is tempting for humans to emphasize competition, and there are times when those dynamics are relevant. But because cooperation is already so embedded in our lives, we tend to underestimate its importance. Even as I type this, I am surrounded by cooperation in both human and systemic forms. The power cord to my computer is providing energy in electron form. The tomato bush on my patio is providing energy in the form of nourishment. Perhaps most importantly, the vast network of family and friends and colleagues surrounding me is providing all sorts of different support. And in turn, I am supporting all of these elements: I pay my electric bill, I water the tomato plant and sing happy songs to it, I support family and friends and colleagues in both tangible and intangible ways.

Sure, I have ongoing debates, disagreements, and certain kinds of competition every single day in my investment work. And I may on occasion swoop in to secure a prime Beacon Hill parking spot ahead of other seekers. But these moments of competition are all embedded in—and enabled by—a huge support system that is intensely cooperative. The cooperative system dwarfs the competitive one; it's just quieter, so we don't always focus on it.

Finally, we need to consider that being locally attuned is a **dynamic, responsive process.** As noted above, functioning feedback loops require accurate signals, effective sensors, and appropriate response. In some ways, it seems our human feedback loops are surely becoming more efficient: we are constantly presented with more data, quicker news flow, and easier response mechanisms. But we don't need to rely on technology. The same sort of dynamic process is embedded in procedures like New England town meetings, where open discussion provides a naturally flexible and evolving set of inputs for governance. Anyone who's gone to such a meeting can attest that they are not always speedy, but they are certainly locally attuned.

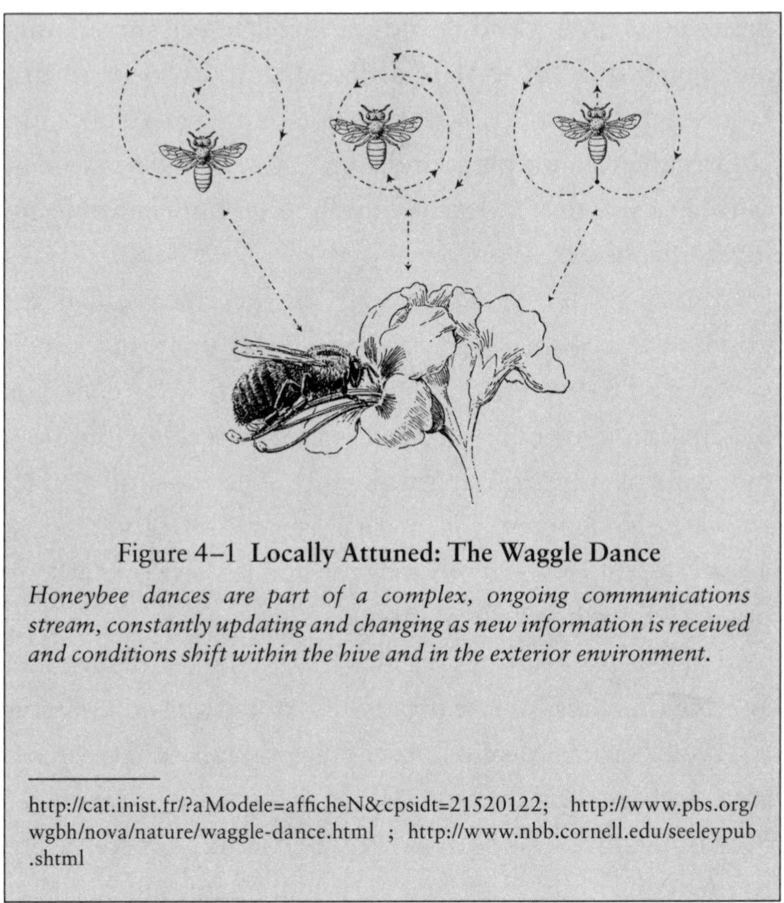

Figure 4–1 **Locally Attuned: The Waggle Dance**

Honeybee dances are part of a complex, ongoing communications stream, constantly updating and changing as new information is received and conditions shift within the hive and in the exterior environment.

---

http://cat.inist.fr/?aModele=afficheN&cpsidt=21520122; http://www.pbs.org/wgbh/nova/nature/waggle-dance.html ; http://www.nbb.cornell.edu/seeleypub.shtml

Translation to Investing

Investing constantly presents chances to create attuned and responsive processes, though we don't always succeed. Take the simple investment example of quarterly earnings releases. In theory, this could be an example of a process that is well aligned with the principles of being locally attuned and responsive. Compiling the results mainly consists of using facts and figures already at hand—readily available materials. And the intention is for investors to better understand what's happening at the company—cultivating cooperative relationships. The activity happens every quarter, so it's clearly a cyclic process. The resulting conversations and changes in security prices could provide useful feedback loops.

Examining one particular company helps to bridge from this theoretically aligned process to the reality of lived experience. When I started covering General Electric in the early 1990s, the press release each quarter consisted of a half page of numbers—revenues, net income, earnings per share, and share count—and a brief comment on performance from then-CEO Jack Welch. After some time a third section was added, including operating summaries for each big division of the company. On days when earnings reports were due, GE analysts all over the world would hover by their fax machines, hoping to be among the first to interpret the results.

These days the quarterly earnings releases from GE (and all other public companies) have ballooned: the latest basic GE earnings report is eleven pages of small print, and the supplemental data packet is thirty-six pages long. These documents are available instantly to anyone with an Internet connection, and are accompanied by detailed slide presentations and a long, recorded conference call.[5] Every possible fact and figure is compiled, under the widely held (and legally enforced) notion that more is better, and that the volume of disclosure is somehow related to the quality of a business. What started as a quick, simple feedback loop has taken on weight and complication that may not serve its intended purpose. A thorough analyst has to spend hours and hours to understand just one set of reports like this from one large company, diverting all of that time and energy from other research that might be longer term or more creative in nature.

At the same time that input volume has skyrocketed, the response mechanisms in investment feedback loops have become much quicker and more automated. Instead of walking over to the trading desk or calling a broker to place an order, you can buy or sell stocks with the click of a button. Even quicker, you can set up trading programs with simple flags so that if phrases like "lowered guidance" or "weak margins" appear in a press release, a stock is automatically sold, without any human intervention.

So, our inputs are greater, processing is faster, and responses are easier. This sounds like great progress in all three areas of investment feedback loops. Quite the contrary. Volume, speed, and ease are not what make for effective feedback loops. In all of our endeavors, including investing, we need relevant information, effective processing, and appropriate response. Instead of "more, faster, easier" we need "relevant, effective, appropriate."

Natural Scorecard: Global Commodities Markets

When we think about "life in context" for our ever more global financial markets, it's clearly important to define that context. What does "local" mean if your business crosses international borders every day? Commodities markets are a curious hybrid, simultaneously local and global: the physical assets are often produced in very concentrated regions (think of aluminum smelters or orange groves), but their distribution covers a much wider area, and their corresponding financial instruments and markets are among the most global of all securities.

Commodities markets have served some of the same purposes of paper currency over the longer term; both have allowed exchange across much greater distances than would be possible if we were hauling actual tons of aluminum to and fro. This is a huge benefit, especially if, say, you run a large baking company and you don't want your business to be subject to the whims of short-term changes in one area's wheat pricing.

This is what I would call the "local" version of commodities markets—people and companies who use the actual products being traded in the course of their own endeavors. Simply speaking, these participants are known as commercial traders. In this context, commercial is the equivalent of local: even though the activity might span great geographic distances, it is a directly connected system, where users and producers of the commodity are the ones engaged in the market. In biological terms this might be analogous to a migratory bird, like the alpine swift. These tiny birds breed in Europe but they winter thousands of miles away in west Africa, where the swifts stay aloft for six months at a time.[6] The "native habitat" of this bird crisscrosses thousands of miles, but when put together, all of those miles form one coherent, connected system.

Commercial commodity participants made up the bulk of commodities trading well into the 1990s. In 1998, physical hedgers (people and organizations that dealt with the actual, tangible commodities) comprised 77 percent of market activity.[7] How do these commercially centered commodities markets stack up against the principles of being locally attuned and responsive?

- **Does it use readily available materials and energy?** A healthy commodities market requires far less energy than a purely physical market. Instead of moving wheat across the country, your western bushels can be matched up with bushels that are closer to an eastern buyer.
- **Does it cultivate cooperative relationships?** All markets are essentially cooperative relationships—every buyer needs a seller. We often frame trading activities as hypercompetitive, but while the search for a single great trading "win" might feel competitive, the market itself is inherently a cooperative endeavor.
- **Does it leverage cyclic processes?** Effective commodities markets are designed to do just this, distributing more complete information that should even out the dramatic swings in price that otherwise occur from region to region, from planting to harvest, from year to year.
- **Use feedback loops—info flows.** This is one of the main goals of commercial commodity markets, to provide more complete information and more accurate, effective feedback loops. If you were a farmer in Illinois in the 1800s and your county had a great corn crop, the price you received

was probably down, even if three counties over there was a drought and record-high prices. With effective commodities markets, a more accurate view of outputs and availability should help both buyers and sellers.

In its essential, user-oriented form, a healthy commodities market matches the natural principles of attunement pretty well. Probably a B-plus, or even an A-minus.

As with all markets, though, expansion in commodities has brought challenges. For entities that actually use aluminum or corn in their business, we can see how commodities markets provide helpful tools. But what about entities that do not use any aluminum in their business, yet participate in the same financial markets as those that do?

Here we hit a slippery slope, the slope between business management, investing, and speculation. In the context of food commodities, speculation is especially important, due to the different functions and flexibilities of food versus, say, metals. If copper prices are very high, construction projects get delayed, inventories are depleted, new sources of supply and substitute materials are sought. Usually, eventually, those adjustments recalibrate prices, and anything that was delayed can be resumed. But if corn prices are very high, people go hungry—and it's no comfort that prices might come down in a few weeks or a few months. The hunger is real, and it's now. This intersection between natural systems, financial systems, and social systems is complex and vital, in ways that do not seem well reflected in our regulatory, operating, or analytical processes.

Here is a simplified summary of changes in commodities trading in recent years:

- Derivatives activity in commodities markets rose steadily through the 1990s and became a source of concern for the Commodity Futures Trading Commission (CTFC).[8]
- However, rather than increasing restrictions, in 2000, the Commodity Futures Modernization Act was passed, which exempted certain markets (such as energy futures) from CFTC oversight.
- The Gramm, Leach, Bliley Act was passed around the same time, which allowed all sorts of new financial players to participate in commodity markets.
- The Chicago Board of Trade (CBOT), the primary agricultural exchange in the United States, raised speculative limits on grain and oilseed contracts too.
- Encouragement for the idea of "commodities as an asset class" rose in both academic and financial circles, which contributed to a rise in commodity index funds from $13 billion in 2003 to $317 billion in 2008.[9] By 2008 it is estimated that these funds accounted for 41 percent of open long interest in commodities markets.[10]
- Perhaps as important as the data above, the perceptions of many participants in food commodities markets seem to have shifted as well. Whereas many individuals involved in these markets historically had some sort of personal

> tie to agriculture, or at least direct knowledge of how their markets linked to the world, a senior exchange official was quoted in 2010 as saying, "I view what we're working with as widgets."[11] In my experience, this disconnected point of view is very common.

To be sure, most of the time, most of what's happening with commodity prices can still be explained by underlying supply–demand dynamics. But what about when speculation is a factor, what happens then? Examining food commodities in particular provides a fascinating and troubling set of answers.

For food commodities, we generally have a long-term backdrop of rising demand due to population growth and global wealth increases, plus some natural limits on arable land and production levels. This combination of rising demand and somewhat limited supply would tend to make long-term prices rise. Supply and demand are just as relevant for food commodities as they are for any other market, and before 2000, supply/demand-based economic models provided strong, fairly complete explanations of food prices.

However, in recent years the proportion of the change in food prices that can be explained solely by supply and demand has been shrinking, indicating that there must be other factors at play. Specifically, as shown by researchers at the New England Complex Systems Institute (NECSI), since 2000, two additional elements have risen in importance when it comes to explaining food commodity prices: ethanol, and deregulation.[12] Ethanol policy has increased demand for corn, which creates upward price pressure for both corn and related crops. And as noted above, deregulation had two types of influences: first, it has made it possible for more and more investors to participate in commodities markets, and second, it has made speculation easier.

Still, why should we care if speculation is causing price spikes? It's not like we go to the store to buy bushels of corn. Oh, wait, we do. As Michael Pollan has highlighted, more than one-quarter of items in our supermarkets contain corn, often in the form of corn syrup, corn-fed chicken and beef, and corn oil.[13] There is a tangible and direct link from this speculative activity to our consumer experience.

Even more interesting than higher prices at the supermarket checkout line—and far more concerning—is mounting evidence that commodity price swings contribute to social unrest. A recent study from the same team at NECSI explains the link between food commodities and public violence. As you'd expect, there are many underlying factors that contribute to social unrest, such as poverty and social injustice. But this study found that high food prices, and especially high and volatile food prices, made violent outbreaks more likely.[14]

This research highlights several important contributing layers to analyze. First, we have created enabling conditions for dysfunction in the structure of our underlying food system: many countries are more reliant on the global markets now, whereas historically local supply and subsistence farming provided buffers to global volatility. Second, we have n-term, structural price pressures on corn due to government policy, particularly ethanol requirements. And finally, we have introduced significant speculative activity, which has extended price spikes beyond what a nonspeculative, supply and demand–driven market would produce.

This combination of factors, and especially the spike in speculation, is clearly tied to social unrest. In other words, the actions of corn speculators in Chicago are directly linked to food riots in Egypt, Libya, and Syria. These riots caused deaths of thousands of people in 2011.[15] One could argue, as noted earlier, that speculation in something like penny stocks is "just a game," where the impacts, though direct, are fairly limited in scope. But speculation in food commodities markets casts a long shadow. It causes hunger, suffering, and violence. As John Fullerton, founder of the Capital Institute notes, "Commodity market manipulation is fundamentally different and far more dangerous than the garden-variety manipulation of financial markets such as in single stock pump and dump schemes, or even the brazen manipulation of LIBOR. Nobody eats LIBOR."[16]

An examination of current food commodity markets, influenced by legislation, regulation, and speculation, reveals a system much less in alignment with the "life in context" principles:

- **Does it use readily available materials and energy?** There is a sort of "false energy" being pulled into commodity markets due to the expansion of external factors like ethanol legislation and financial speculation. These influences are less and less connected with the core function of commodities and the original function of their markets.

- **Does it cultivate cooperative relationships?** The fundamental cooperative nature of markets has been distorted here by a three-in-one combined commodities market function: we have the core commercial market, the legislatively induced market, and the speculative market. Each set of participants has different needs and motivations, which are disconnected and out of sync with one another. This is fundamentally a fragile and volatile system.
- **Does it leverage cyclic processes?** Relationship of commodity markets to the natural cycles of crop growing is more and more distant, due to the expanded market participants and purposes.
- **Does it use effective feedback loops?** Feedback loops are distorted by these same market extensions, rendering correction mechanisms less effective as well.

Not only does speculation amplify price swings, and not only do those price swings increase the fragility of our social systems, but that fragility is causing tangible human harm and suffering. We see in the food commodity markets a combination of **market disruption and moral disruption**. This is a dangerous combination, one that demands understanding and correction.

Evolution

It would be easy to overlook one of the most vital elements of the analysis we've referenced in this chapter: the idea that local food systems used to be more robust, and that many parts of the world used to be less reliant on global food commodities than they are today. The effects of the legislation, deregulation, and speculation discussed above would not be so awful if they did not directly impact so many dispersed local systems. So, yes, we likely need to make some major adjustments to commodities markets. But we also need to strengthen the local systems that can buffer impact. It's like building up coastal ecosystems so that there is more shelter from ocean storms.

Luckily, there is a lot of vibrant local investing activity, and much of it is particularly focused on nurturing and strengthening local food systems. For example, the Slow Money movement focuses on "bringing money back to earth" and "investing as if food, farms, and fertility mattered."[17] Numerous local chapters have emerged to provide on-the-ground focus in their own regions through investing, education, and support for local entrepreneurs. I belong to a lending group in Boston that is affiliated with our local Slow Money organization and it has proven to be a great way to better understand and invest in our local food system, to meet real live farmers and entrepreneurs who help to nourish that system, and perhaps most importantly, to work with other local friends toward shared benefit for our community.

The Business Alliance for Local Living Economies (BALLE) focuses on creating prosperity through vibrant local economies and communities, with eighty local business networks and a broad offering of opportunities for education, connection, and investment.[18] I admire that the BALLE localism movement focuses on the entire system, recognizing that energy, food, business, and community are all inextricably linked, and that to focus on a single element in isolation will not enable full-system prosperity.

Finally, community development financial institutions (CDFIs), over one thousand-strong in the United States, continue to provide crucial small business funding in many communities. As a group, CDFIs grew lending and credit union assets faster than traditional counterparts straight through the late-2000s' financial downturn.[19]

These three are just a few examples of a broader wave of local engagement that can be witnessed in political, social, and economic contexts across the globe. And many of these endeavors are supported by the simpler, more direct mechanisms that form the basis of transformation from synthetic to simplified. We can start to see how these transformations intertwine and reinforce each other, forming the basis of a healthier investing ecosystem.

Pathway to Practice

How can we move toward investing that is more connected, more in context? Nature's principles of local attunement offer a path.

In natural terms, local often means nearby. But even more than that, it means connected. First think of the literal meaning of local. Is some of your investing centered in your own community? Are there ways to connect your resources more with your local life? Then think of the more metaphorical "local," that is, connected. When you look at your account statements, do you know what's in those funds? Do you know the products that the companies produce? Can you explain the details of each security? You don't need to know every detail of every investment (though that is a noble goal), but if you don't even recognize most of the listings on your own account statements, it might be time to sift through to see which are really serving valuable purposes and which are more speculative, or just "fillers."

When I think of the house building work I've done with Habitat for Humanity, I am struck by the many layers of connection that are present: connection to place, connection to community, connection to mission, and connection of people across all sorts of possible divisions—religious, political, and national. Unfortunately, I still don't see this kind of connection present in all of my own investing, but I am more and more focused on identifying it and pursuing it. If I can't describe how my investment is visible in the world, that's one strike. If I can't explain its direct and indirect effects (hopefully benefits) in some detail, that's two strikes. If I can't even explain how it works, that's three strikes—out. By filtering my investing through these questions, I am trying to move my investing bit by bit from **transactional to relational.**

Sowing Seeds of Locally Attuned Investing

Here are some ways to move from transactional to relational investing, to focus on investing that thrives in context:

- **Define context.** Decide what constitutes the context of your investing. Maybe you want to focus on a certain set of themes or a type of organization, a geographic region, or a type of security. Define what is "local" to you.
- **Cultivate cooperation.** Try to back off the alpha tendencies for just a moment, and recognize that we are surrounded and supported by cooperative systems. Competition can be helpful, but it floats in a massive sea of cooperation, and it need not be a zero sum game. Are there ways to achieve your purpose that do not involve crushing someone else? There probably are. Better yet, could you achieve your purpose by *supporting* someone else? I bet you could.
- **Create dynamic/responsive—healthy feedback loops.** What information are you monitoring for your investments? Feedback loops need to include relevant information, effective processing, and appropriate response. What kinds of feedback will let you know what's really happening, and if adjustments are needed? Daily price reports and constant investment turnover are not likely to be the most useful inputs.

As we attune to our own contexts, our local environments, our investing naturally becomes more connected.

We can eliminate harmful, needless speculation, and focus on investments that are valued and valuable to both parties.

We can recognize the ubiquitous cooperative systems that enable our small moments of competition.

We can move from disconnected to reconnected.

Transformation 5

From Mechanical to Mindful

"You're right on the line!" an agitated audience member proclaimed. I had just presented results for the mid-cap funds I was managing to a big group of financial advisors.

"Ummm, what line?" I asked, a little bit confused. The backdrop to these meetings was a positive one: the funds were doing well, and so was the overall stock market (this was the late 1990s), so it was unusual to meet an unhappy investor. My first alarming thought was that he meant some sort of ethical line, or a personal one—that he did not approve of some of the fund's holdings, or thought I had invested too much in technology stocks.

"This one!" he poked his finger at a set of papers. It was not a metaphorical limit he meant—it was an actual line, the line in the Morningstar chart that placed my fund in the mid-cap growth box. Sure enough, my fund was right on the edge between "blend" and "growth."

"I have to sell your fund if you cross the line," he explained, eyes wide. "Don't cross the line." It turned out that his firm had a strict asset allocation policy, so that if

my fund moved from one box to another, he would indeed have to sell it.

"Well, I'm just buying the best mid-cap stocks I find," I replied, trying to emphasize that my responsibility was to shareholders and not to the chart he held. He turned away in frustration, shaking his head.

This was my first clue that our assessment tools had taken on a life of their own. They had begun to influence our practices and cause us to adapt, but not in a healthy or intended way.

Nature's Principle: Adapt to Changing Conditions

Adaptation is a curious concept for investors: we want to be nimble and to be able to adjust as the environment shifts, but we also want to be consistent and reliable. The detail behind the natural principle **adapt to changing conditions** acknowledges that we live in a world that is constantly in flux and illustrates that adaptation is not just about any old response. It's the appropriateness of response that matters, the way that the response is triggered and managed. Proper adaptation requires designs and processes that are inherently dynamic, not static. The subprinciples of adaptation are:

- Maintain integrity through self-renewal.
- Embody resilience through variation, redundancy, and decentralization.
- Incorporate diversity.

The first element of adaptability is the ability to **maintain integrity through self-renewal.** What does this mean? Persistence! Perseverance! Adaptable organisms are constantly adding energy and resources to heal and improve the system, on both micro and macro levels. Think of a tree that loses a big branch in a snowstorm—if it's healthy, by the next spring you'll usually start to see new branches forming near the lost limb. Or consider our own bodies, healing cuts by marshaling all sorts of different resources to clot the blood, fight infection, and form new skin and scar tissue around the wound. Self-renewal is the process of maintaining integrity, not of holding a rigid form constant in the face of change.

Adaptation also requires **embodied resilience.** It's not enough to be resilient only in theory: this quality must be actively demonstrated and fostered through **variation, redundancy, and decentralization.** The quirky little sea slug called a nudibranch shows how these qualities are positive and necessary. Obviously, a slug is a vulnerable creature—slow moving and unprotected, offering a squishy, easy meal for predators. To protect themselves, nudibranchs are often crazily, garishly colored, alerting predators to toxicity. In a stunning show of adaptation, the source of this toxicity is directly related to the nudibranch's particular environment: for example, many varieties protect themselves by eating toxic substances like the stinging cells from jellyfish tentacles or anemones. Instead of being poisoned themselves, the nudibranchs pass the toxins through to harm would-be predators. Other sorts of nudibranchs, rather than sporting loud colors of warning, take on the color of their own food sources—so, for example, one feeding on coral will be coral colored, invisible to attackers. These adaptations to local food sources allow the nudibranch to thrive in shifting (and threatening) conditions.[1]

A glance at sea slug photos (really, take a look!) reveals stunning variation within the species, while the multiple mechanisms for "borrowing" toxins from other creatures demonstrate redundancy. The way that adjustments are localized to each particular environmental setting reflects decentralization. Those three characteristics—variation, redundancy, and decentralization—tend to have a negative tone in business settings, where we often aim for consistency, efficiency, and centralization. But resilience is every investor's dream: to be able to prosper in a range of changing environments, with all sorts of resource shifts and a wide mix of neighbors, some with friendly intentions and some more predatory.

The final component of adaptability, **diversity**, might at first seem to be the same as variation, discussed above. However, while variation refers to the mix of organisms, diversity refers to the mix of forms, processes, or systems that exist to perform a particular function. Variation is a mixture of "what," but in this context, diversity is a mixture of "how." In a forest, we can easily see the distinction: trees can regenerate through internal growth, seedling growth, or new shoots from old roots. Water capture can come from root systems, geographic features, or built structures. There are many different trees (variation), and also many ways for regeneration and water capture to occur (diversity).

Three key themes are embedded within the natural

principles of adaptation. First, the concept of **self-renewal as a dynamic cycle.** Perhaps I am over-conditioned by years of exposure to women's magazines, but when I see "self-renewal," I tend to think of "antiaging" or turning back the clock. That association is completely misplaced in the context of biomimicry. Here, self-renewal does not imply going back to some prior form; rather it's a tool for healing, change, and improvement. Going forward.

Luckily, outside the realm of beauty creams, this sort of self-renewal is a familiar idea. For example, education and training are forms of self-renewal, adding energy and resources to acquire new knowledge and capabilities. One of the most common aspirations in the business community is to be part of a "learning organization." Similarly, Charlie Munger, Warren Buffett's longtime business partner, often discusses his efforts to build diverse "mental models," so that he has intellectual frameworks that help to navigate a wide range of situations. Early in his career, Munger realized that this self-renewal was so important that he decided to bill an hour a day to himself, so that he could invest the time in projects that interested him, rather than projects other people paid him to do.[2] Whether physical, emotional, spiritual, or intellectual, these types of personal investments in renewal are all ways to build adaptive capacity.

Resilience is also a commonly confused term: the perception is that resilience means "bouncing back," but the concept is more nuanced than that. In biological terms, resilience is about *maintaining function* in light of disturbance—not retaining form, not recovering to an original state. Within nature's principles, **resilience is explicitly**

multidimensional, incorporating variation, redundancy, and decentralization.

Those resilient qualities might sound fine for a forest, but in many human endeavors it's not so clear that they're desirable. In business, "redundancy" is usually a synonym for "waste." Indeed, in human resources circles, when you are "made redundant," it does not mean you've won a prize for your contributions to resilience; it means you've been fired. We tend to view the main mechanisms of resilience—variation, redundancy, decentralization—as enemies of efficiency. In our quest for efficiency in human endeavors, we can decrease resilience.

The third embedded concept in the adaptation principles is that **diversity is an asset.** This might be well understood in some organizational settings, but it is very rarely acknowledged in process design, where our assumption is that standardization is the best approach. There are a few specialties that value diversity, like airplane safety or nuclear engineering, where we want multiple options for landing the plane or shutting down a reactor core. But these are the exceptions, not the rule, and even then, we usually choose a mix of standardized options. Diversity of mechanisms is the exact opposite of standardization, and it is standardization that's been the hallmark of our business practices since the days of Henry Ford. Of course, standardization might be well suited for assembly lines, with predictable work flows and homogeneous products, but we have misapplied it to many endeavors like investing, where conditions, products, and processes are constantly in flux.

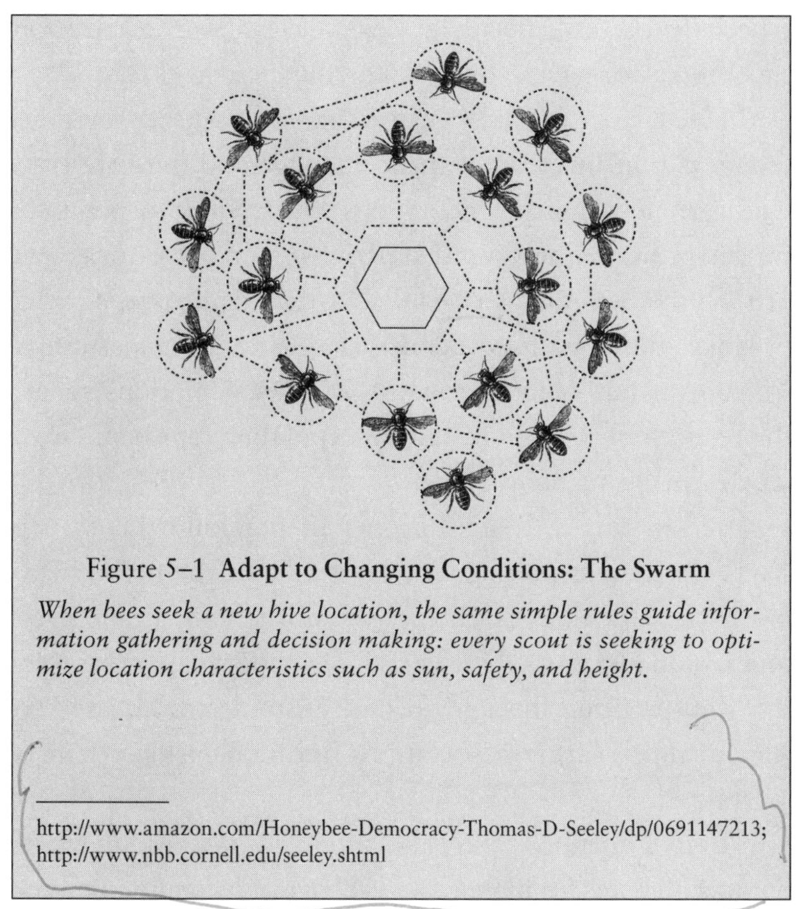

Figure 5–1 **Adapt to Changing Conditions: The Swarm**

When bees seek a new hive location, the same simple rules guide information gathering and decision making: every scout is seeking to optimize location characteristics such as sun, safety, and height.

---

http://www.amazon.com/Honeybee-Democracy-Thomas-D-Seeley/dp/0691147213; http://www.nbb.cornell.edu/seeley.shtml

Translation to Investing

The qualities of natural adaptability are not always embraced in business, but they still seem like no-brainers when it comes to investing. We all recognize the inherent risks and uncertainties presented by a changing economic and investing environment, and the qualities of adaptability (and especially of resilience) represent a clear way to develop capabilities for navigating that changing environment.

Indeed, the premise behind most modern portfolio theory is that investors want to manage and mitigate risk. Unfortunately, as the theory has been put into practice, we have increasingly used narrow quantitative measures of risk like beta and VaR (value at risk) as proxies for the broader, more qualitative concepts of risk and uncertainty. This mismatch—the narrowness of the calculations versus the breadth and depth of the concepts they represent—can have devastating consequences.[3]

Even in this one small corner of portfolio theory, we see two different problematic layers. First, the mechanical layer: the calculations themselves are very narrow, each focused on just one subset of risk. Second, the human layer: this data is often misapplied and misunderstood, used to leap to much larger associations and conclusions than is warranted.

Though intended to explain and to control risk, many of our mechanisms for managing risk have only focused on very narrow, short-term measures. These tools have not improved long-term risk management, and have not increased adaptability; instead, they have unwittingly decreased it, by establishing more and more structured approaches that inherently have less variation, less diversity, less flexibility. We have chosen rigidity instead of responsiveness, in the hope that the walls of ever more solid structures and processes will repel risk and uncertainty at the perimeters of our endeavors. We have sought control—an impossible goal—instead of aiming for adaptability and resilience.

Natural Scorecard: Mutual Funds and Their Analytics

At first glance, mutual funds seem to be among the slower-moving organisms within the investment world. The structure of these products has been pretty constant for the last seventy-five years, and they rarely carry the same sizzle in the headlines as high-frequency trading or hedge funds do. But this underlying stability of form is exactly what makes mutual funds the perfect illustration of misdirected adaptation in our investment practices. The funds themselves have changed much less quickly than their ecosystem—the tools, policies, and procedures that surround them.

The steadiness in form also reflects a steadiness in **function** for mutual funds: far and away, their main function in the investment ecosystem is to provide diversification for investors. After all, it is a *mutual* fund! The whole point of a mutual fund is that people are coming together to share in both risks and returns. In natural terms, a mutual fund allows investors to invest in a small piece of a whole forest, instead of owning just one tree or a colony of beetles or a few acorns.

The principles of adaptability were easy to observe in fund management for more than fifty years. As recently as the early 1990s, the most common type of mutual fund was a "go-anywhere" fund, where the portfolio manager had wide discretion over where to invest shareholders' money. If large-cap U.S. stocks looked attractive, they might be a fund's largest holdings. If the manager believed there was more opportunity in small international companies, she could invest there instead, without extra permissions or external approvals or fear of "crossing the line."

How does the basic mutual fund structure hold up to the standards of adaptation?

- **Does it adapt to changing conditions? Is it *appropriately* reactive?** A fund can self-renew by redeploying assets from one holding to another—though whether reactions are appropriate depends on the manager and the circumstances.
- **Does it maintain integrity through self-renewal?** A fund can demonstrate resilience through variation, redundancy, and decentralization of its holdings. As one of my early mentors said, "The greatest thing about fund management is, when things change, you can change your mind."[4]
- **Does it embody resilience? Does it value effectiveness over efficiency? Does it incorporate diversity?** Yes, a fund can incorporate diversity by holding multiple types of securities and multiple types of businesses.

The fundamental structure of mutual funds is pretty well aligned with natural principles of adaptability—somewhere around an A-minus. But as the number of mutual funds grew, so did the need to distinguish one fund from another. One essential challenge was sheer volume—variation, as defined in our principles above. An individual investor might be expected to sort through a few dozen options to make a reasonable choice, but several thousand? With more than three thousand U.S. mutual funds by 1990 (up from 564 in 1980), there were practical and serious issues of navigation that needed to be addressed.[5]

Another challenge at this time was variability: not only were there many funds in number (variation), but their results were also quite disparate (variability). Fund investors were being called upon to navigate a more and more complex landscape, but without many maps or tools to assist them.

With the proliferation in numbers of mutual funds and dispersion of their results, the stage was set for the development of tools to sort through all of that data. One early example of a tool for fund analysis is the investment style box, pioneered and popularized by Morningstar. This simple three-by-three grid sketches out categories for small-, mid-, and large-cap funds on the vertical axis, with value, blend, and growth styles across the horizontal axis.

Here is a quick review of the evolution of this one investment tool:

- The **style box tool** was developed in 1992 by Morningstar. Early on, the style boxes fulfilled their role exactly as designed: thousands of mutual funds on jumbled-up lists were sorted into straightforward categories, based not on what their names implied but on the data of their actual holdings. This was a huge service: now it was easy to tell which "large-cap" funds were secretly full of $300 million retail stocks and which "value" funds were full of high-flying biotech holdings.
- The tool had (and has) **clear and legitimate function.** Morningstar's own advice notes: "How lines are drawn among value, blend, and growth is somewhat arbitrary, and it is perfectly acceptable for a fund manager to invest in a range of styles. The Style Box tool provides a context for understanding the holdings, not a constraint."[6]

• However, **misplaced feedback loops** began to take hold, and the tool began to influence decision making in an unintended way, as noted in this chapter's opening story. A study published in 2003 found that changes in Morningstar assessments had independent abnormal effects on fund flows (that is, effects independent of other performance variables) of 13 to 30 percent.[7]

• These style boxes have become such **standardized tools** that they are increasingly used as part of the default construct for asset management. This is one factor leading to the popularity of "target date" funds, a type of auto-adjusting portfolio that shifts assets between categories according to the shareholder's stage of life. This type of fund had just under $50 billion in assets at the end of 2002, and mushroomed to approach $800 billion in assets at the end of 2012.[8]

Unintentionally, what started out as a needed and helpful tool began to influence decision making in inappropriate ways. In this regard, the Morningstar boxes are just one example of a much broader and deeper trend. When we assess a mutual fund model that is heavily tools-influenced, we see much less adaptability:

• **Does it adapt to changing conditions? Is it *appropriately* reactive?** The more narrow a fund's mandate (whether intentional or unintentional), the fewer opportunities there are for it to adapt.

• **Does it maintain integrity through self-renewal?** It is more and more difficult for a fund manager to change her mind. Most funds are now managed by a combination of committees and computers, which dampens the opportunity for individual creativity and responsiveness.

• **Does it embody resilience? Does it value effectiveness over efficiency? Does it incorporate diversity?** Again, a fund manager who is trying to stay "in the box" is by definition constrained.

During this tool-influenced era, discussions of businesses and products and whether they made for good investments have given way to discussions of tracking error, active bets, and portfolio construction. But the latter conversations rarely link those risk measures back to actual investments in the funds, or link those investments in turn to what is happening in the real world. We are increasingly **attempting to manage risk by measuring it**, and in proper context this might be a helpful endeavor. However, our measurements are less and less connected to tangible activity in the world, and thus we are less and less well equipped to take appropriate action. Our investment dollars are clearly reflecting a desire to manage and minimize risk and uncertainty, but they are also reflecting a desire to automate those processes, to avoid thinking about them. And with everyone using the same tools, resilience of the overall system is undermined.

This maladaptation of our funds and tools highlights an important paradox: one of the greatest conditions for resilience (variation of organisms) can also be related to conditions that are unappealing to investors (variability in results). How can we reconcile the high degree of dispersion that a resilient system implies with our desire for consistency?

To help sort out this paradox, it's important to

distinguish between two distinct elements, **risk and uncertainty.** Most of our tools are intended to help us understand variation (the range of elements) and manage variability (the range of results). The first part, understanding variation, is pretty well addressed by popular analytical methods.

But variability—breadth of results—is a lot tougher to understand, and even more difficult to manage. Variability has two components. The first is *risk*—where the range of possibilities is known but the outcome is not clear. The second is *uncertainty*—where neither the range of possibilities nor the outcome is known. This distinction between risk and uncertainty was documented by Frank Knight in the 1920s, and has been well illustrated more recently by Michael Mauboussin, amongst others.[9] Think of risk as a question of where results fall along a normal distribution. Think of uncertainty as a situation where results fall in a huge, wide-open space.

If you illustrate these two pictures with hand gestures you can actually feel how different the challenges are: risk is a complicated but tidy mathematical exercise, while uncertainty is the great unknown. Really, try it. Put this book down and make these forms in the air. Risk . . . a nice, steady curve. Uncertainty . . . a wild flailing and flapping around. See? This is not a geeky irrelevant distinction—these are fundamentally different concepts.

Here is the tough part: we can model risk until the cows come home, but there are no good models for uncertainty; in fact, that is the definition of uncertainty, that it is not model-able. And that—let's admit it—is terrifying. So as we've employed our ever-larger risk-management tool kits, it's been easy to pretend that they work for uncertainty too. But they don't.

Even worse, when we use ever more stringent mechanisms to control risk, we undermine exactly the characteristics that are needed to withstand uncertainty. When we limit creativity on the part of fund managers, our intention is to reduce risk, but instead we limit adaptation. When we create funds of funds like those target-date offerings, our intention is to reduce risk, but in doing so, we limit diversity. When we increase regulation and distribution, our intention is to reduce risk, but instead we increase centralization.

Our efforts to control risk have been in direct conflict with building an adaptive, resilient system.

Evolution

When I survey the investing landscape, I'm encouraged to see more and more "unboxed" investment approaches springing up. Some of these are occurring in the social investing, impact investing, and patient capital arenas, where the lines between philanthropy and investing are more and more blurred. Organizations like Acumen are pioneering "first loss" investments with philanthropic dollars, which allow more traditional investors to collaborate more easily on innovative social business ventures. Numerous family foundations have decided to deploy *all* of their assets toward their missions, not just the 5 percent they'd normally give away in grants each year. Discussions of "full-spectrum" investing have flipped their focus, from centering on what vehicle to use—that is, what box to choose—to what outcomes are sought—that is, what kind of world we want to foster with our efforts.

Some sense of the energy—and chaos—surrounding these unboxed investment approaches can be gained by observing the SoCap conference, held every fall in San Francisco. Topics range from gender lens investing to ocean-related endeavors to urban innovation to partnerships with indigenous communities.... In short, everything that you likely won't find on your 401(k) form. Yet. In one short hour at the conference this year, I ran into friends from my biomimicry class, a spiritual conscious investing group, a women's research project, a local food–advocacy organization, and a good old-fashioned venture capital firm. My mentor Susan Davis always advises that to start a revolution, you should throw a better party, and gatherings like SoCap are definitely more fun than most traditional Wall Street conferences are these days.

One critique of impact investing and other innovative approaches is that they sometimes appear to be clubs that are closed to all but the very wealthy, due to curious laws that are intended to "protect" others from taking too much risk with their money. Thankfully, many people are not daunted by this set of structures, and are finding ways to invest "out of the box" with whatever mechanisms make sense. The Transition Movement is helping local communities invest in a carbon-free future.[10] Farmer's markets and community agriculture programs are seeing record growth throughout the United States. Gift giving increasingly includes free-trade goods, charitable donations, or personal experiences, instead of mass-produced stuff. None of these activities fits on the Morningstar grid, and that's exactly the point.

Pathway to Practice

Our search for resilience in portfolio management has been replaced by the partial—and often false—comfort of "risk management." Yet within that misdirected journey, we can still dig back to the roots, identifying helpful starting points to set us on a more adaptable course. And then we can send up shoots, beginning to take steps along a different, more resilient pathway of practice.

The first step on that more resilient pathway is to **refocus the questions** we are trying to answer and to expand them to their higher level of significance. We do not need to ask why the tracking error for any given mutual fund changed by 0.1 in the latest quarter; we need to ask whether we are building adaptable, resilient products and systems. This shift in focus is like tending the garden versus being constantly in harvest mode.

Most importantly, we need to consider how to **prepare for uncertainty**, and to acknowledge that this preparation might include things that appear inefficient—or even risky—in the short term. Preparing for uncertainty connects with all the principles of adaptation that we've discussed in this chapter: investing in renewal, variation, redundancy, decentralization, and diversity. This preparation is like planting fruit trees that will benefit your children more than yourself, or adding a few drought-tolerant species even if it's raining this week and the risk seems remote.

Once we establish this initial reorientation toward resilience in our investing, other layers of opportunity are revealed. For example, our portfolios should be adaptive and resilient, sure, but isn't one way to accomplish this to invest in other entities that are *themselves* adaptive and resilient enterprises? This is the investing equivalent of planting new seeds, trying new crops. Some will fail, to be sure, but some will flourish.

With this question in mind, we can extend our thinking beyond the current boxes and pie charts, which are mainly comprised of public securities of large institutions plus sometimes an extra wedge for gold or real estate. Once we consider adaptation and resilience seriously, the question is not whether large-cap stocks will outperform small caps, or whether muni bonds will outperform Treasuries. The real question is whether our investing is supporting entities that are themselves resilient, and that are contributing in turn to resilience of life on earth. This is not reflected in any asset allocation pie chart I've seen, nor is it answered by owning a fund of funds.

Many of the tools and processes that have been developed in investing over the last thirty years are rooted in modern portfolio theory. This theory reflects a clear desire to understand, measure, and control risk, but it has some major shortcomings, much like the mutual fund tools we've analyzed in this chapter. Most significantly, it narrows the definitions of risk. This makes it easy to misinterpret various calculations, and to assume they mean much more than they really do.

Employing life's principles helps us to refocus on bigger, more essential questions, and bigger, more essential functions. This in turn enables us to redirect our processes, procedures, and products—to realign them with essential concepts like adaptability and resilience. So instead of asking, what Morningstar box does this fund belong in? Or, what is the Sharpe ratio for this portfolio? We can ask, is this approach adaptable? Does it demonstrate variation, redundancy, and decentralization? Is it reflecting diversity in how form meets function?

Sowing Seeds of Resilience in Your Own Investing

One of the most important words related to the adaptability principles is "appropriate": the goal is *appropriate* reaction to changing conditions. Now that we have examined some of the challenges our current investing has with respect to this principle, what is the appropriate reaction?

- **Consider the distinction between risk and uncertainty** carefully. Be sure to avoid relying on traditional risk tools in situations where the real concern is uncertainty.
- **Use data as information, not as a prescription** for action. Tools are just that—inputs into the decision-making process, not determinants of its outcome.
- **Plan feedback loops that match the intended function**—seek data that demonstrate alignment with adaptability

principles. What's measured should relate to the purpose of the investment, should refresh itself over time, and should be met with an appropriate receptor and reaction.

- **Beware of "duration trading"**—approaches that might decrease short-term risk are tempting, but they also might undermine long-term resilience. Try not to trade one for the other.
- **Invest in variation, redundancy, decentralization, and diversity.**

Like farmers who are fostering resilience by replanting fields with multiple crops, natural windbreaks, and fewer chemical treatments, we can reinvest in adaptation and the roots of resilience: variation, redundancy, decentralization, and diversity.

We can move from rigid processes to responsive ones.

We can shift from mechanical to mindful.

Transformation 6

From Static to Dynamic

It had been a tough morning. Our firm held a stake of several hundred million dollars in one of the stocks I was recommending, and the company's quarterly results had fallen short of expectations. The stock was down more than 10 percent, so we'd lost tens of millions of dollars.

The short-term disruptions at the company were well explained, and most were of a transitory nature: a slipped deadline here, some cost inflation there. Of course, every analyst wonders what she could have done to better anticipate problems like these, but I had analyzed the results carefully and was confident that prospects for the business were still strong. I was recommending that we not just hold the stock but buy more, which is what I conveyed to the manager of the biggest fund at my firm, the one who held the largest position in this stock.

He was not emotional or angry, despite the stock's decline—quarterly results are always volatile, and we'd discussed this company together many times. Plus, every investor eventually learns how to calibrate his emotions, to try to distinguish between "noise" and more serious issues. At the end of our discussion he sighed a little and concluded, "Look, I understand the short-term issues, and I'm not selling the stock. But be careful when you make claims about long term prospects after a quarter like this. The long term is a series of short terms."

Is it true? Is the long term really a series of short terms? Life's principles of evolution show that it is that...and much more.

Nature's Principle: Evolve to Survive

Timing on Wall Street is a tricky thing. Though many investors intend to be long-term in their orientation, we are constantly being pulled back to the day-to-day, minute-to-minute measurement that is now part of investment culture. One colleague of mine who dared to divest his Internet stocks in 1998, long before the dot-com bubble burst, was warned almost daily, "The market can stay irrational longer than you can remain solvent."[1] And indeed, every day that stocks like Webvan and eToys rose was like an eternity for my friend, both in terms of performance for his funds and in terms of the psychic toll that it took to watch those prices soar and soar.

During this same period, another colleague positioned his oversized market screens behind his desk, so he could work with his back to them for most of the day. I loved this idea and tried it eagerly, but I had to put the screens back in front within a few days because my back was so sore. I was spending all of my time twisting around in my chair, mesmerized by the flashing red and green numbers. Much as I thought my decisions were long term, my actions—at least in performance monitoring—were decidedly micro term.

Stretching to embrace the truly long-term view, as required by the natural principle, **evolve to survive**, can feel like an uphill battle for investors who are buffeted by short-termism. Yet when I think of the best investors I know, they have fully embraced this principle, always stretching to incorporate new ideas into their investment practice and always tacking toward the long term, even while immediate issues demand attention too. The long term is a series of short terms, yes, but simply pasting together short-term plans with no longer view will not produce a successful, resilient strategy.

The subprinciples of biomimicry's principle of evolution are:

- Replicate what works.
- Integrate the unexpected.
- Reshuffle information.

What are the components of a durable, evolutionary approach? Three factors come together within this principle to create a resilient strategy: first, **replicate what works**. This is a little like your grandparents' motto, "If it ain't broke, don't fix it." Think of a horseshoe crab—it looks like something that could have roamed around with the dinosaurs, in part because the crab has continued to replicate what works: the hard shell, the multiple eyes, the spiny "horn" for navigating. All of these features have existed (and persisted) for roughly 150 million years because they work.[2]

The flip side of replicating what works is the incorporation of new elements: **integrate the unexpected.** When the option for a new approach arises, it should be explored and, if successful, embodied in practice. An example here would be the snowshoe hare, which has giant back feet with claws that function like snowshoes—perfect for navigating across snowdrifted environments. When those feet first emerged, they were a mutation, one that happened to be especially well suited to the environment at hand. Another mutation allowed the hare to change color, so that it turns bright white in winter and brown-gray in spring, in order to blend in better with its surroundings. Over time the hares with these mutations fared better, and so the mutations gradually "stuck," becoming integrated into the hare's basic design. As habitats are now changing, some studies suggest that these mutations are a liability instead of a benefit, so it remains to be seen how the hares continue to attune in the short term, adapt in the medium term, and evolve in the long term.[3]

The key connector between replicating what works and integrating the unexpected is the ability to **reshuffle information.** Biologically, most of this reshuffling happens via reproduction, where all sorts of cross-pollinations and genetic variations are possible. The relationship between mammoths and elephants over time is a great illustration of information reshuffling; generations of the animal became less and less furry over time as their home climates became warmer and warmer.[4]

For human organizations and processes, these biological principles reflect three important concepts. First is the question of **embodiment**: for evolution to work, new ideas are not just ideas, they are fully incorporated into processes and systems. For many years I lauded the idea of keeping an investment diary, where you set aside time to note important events, your analysis, your emotion, and your decisions. And yet for most of those years, that's all I did—I liked the idea. It wasn't until I actually started keeping such a document that I could see patterns in my own biases and my own analytical tendencies. It was not thinking about this record keeping that helped, or recognizing that it was a good idea; it was the embodiment of this practice that finally led to positive impact.

The second important concept embedded in these principles is the **definition of success**. Natural measures of success are often easy to assess: if an organism survives, it's successful. It's tempting to translate this idea directly to our investment endeavors, to say that we have a "sink or swim" approach for new ideas or methodologies, but that's a little too convenient, especially when our time frame for measurement is often very short. And in fact, to produce successful long-term evolution, we need to accept **gigantic failure rates** along the way. Most mutations are short lived because they provide no benefit, and indeed sometimes they hinder survival instead of helping it. So we need to identify "graceful failure" mechanisms in our endeavors, a way to try new ideas without putting too much weight on their early, risky outcomes.

For example, Peter Lynch, legendary manager of the Fidelity Magellan Fund, often referred to his "farm team" of hundreds of tiny holdings. These holdings were so small that any one of them could not have much impact on the portfolio, good or bad, but having them in the mix allowed these new ideas to be monitored, compared with bigger holdings, and generally "tried out." If they were successful, they could grow to have real positive impact on the portfolio, but if they were unsuccessful, the price of failure was not too high. Though Lynch didn't describe it this way, this practice is a great example of applying evolutionary principles to investing.[5]

However, employing this kind of evolutionary practice in investing is relatively rare, as it is eclipsed by fear. Jeremy Grantham, cofounder and chief investment strategist of Grantham Mayo van Otterloo, often notes that "The central truth of the investment business is that investment behavior is driven by career risk . . . you must never, ever be wrong on your own."[6] This very powerful, very human element of investing puts personal survival ahead of principled long-term thinking. In some ways, this is the most evolutionary approach of all: focus on survival. But focusing on short-term survival as an investor often has the unfortunate consequence of weakening the foundation for long-term survival. Defining success over an appropriate time frame, then, is a difficult and necessary piece of the puzzle.

Finally, the principles of "evolve to survive" weigh in very strongly on the notion of **open versus closed systems**. For many investment organizations, the allure of proprietary approaches looms large. Who wouldn't want a proprietary trading system or a big stack of proprietary research to draw upon? But "evolve to survive" implies that we need to consider our esteem for exclusivity more carefully. For effective evolution, we need to ensure constant pollination of new ideas, and a system that is too closed off and buttoned up simply cannot provide enough of this newness. Even if a closed group can bring in lots of outside data and ideas, if there is no two-way flow, all it can offer in return is payment; there is no deeper exchange. For durable success, we need true exchange, not just paid data transfer. Though it is an uncomfortable shift, many investment organizations need to move from a proprietary, internally focused mind-set to a more open, innovative mind-set: from preservation to renewal.

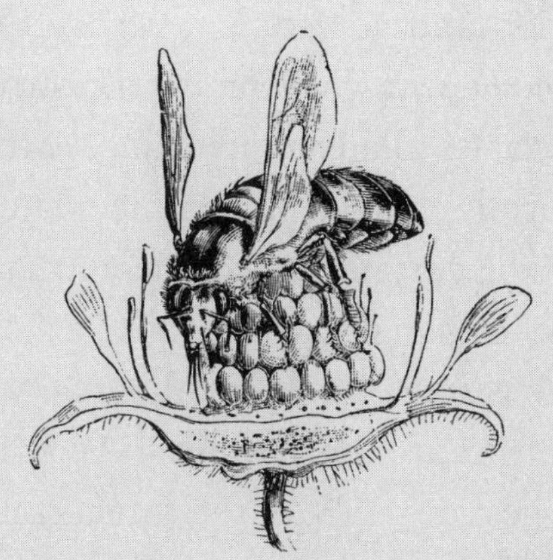

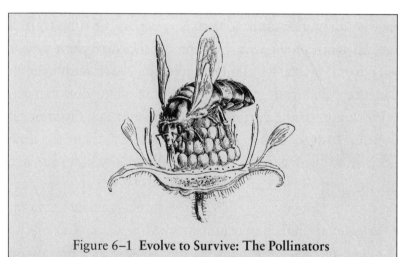

Figure 6–1 **Evolve to Survive: The Pollinators**

The nectar in flowers evolved from ferns, and its sole purpose is to attract pollinators. Likewise, bees evolved to be optimal collectors—a 90mg bee can hold 40mg of nectar.

http://www.guardian.co.uk/environment/2011/apr/04/honeybees-entomb-hives

o Investing

As noted above, it can be hard to consider finance and investing in a truly long-term, evolutionary context: sometimes even thinking beyond the next quarter feels like a curious, old-fashioned sort of thing to do. And yet timing is just as finely calibrated in nature: think of the mouse caught by a snake in just a fraction of a second or an apple tree that blooms just a few days too late for optimal pollination. Nature balances the short term and the long term just as successful investors do.

What is most essential in nature, as well as in investing, is adaptation and adjustment, across all time frames and all sorts of different environments. In fact, three of our six natural principles allude to adjusting, each with its own cadence. "Be locally attuned" is an immediate idea, focused on fitting in to the current environment at any given point in time. "Adapt to changing conditions" lengthens the time horizon to the medium term, explaining how best to thrive as the environment around us shifts. And "evolve to survive" is the longest duration of the three, concentrating on multigenerational change and survival.

Each of these principles references strategies for coping with changing circumstances, and each provides important road maps for investors as well. When it comes to evolution, the essential questions posed to investors are profound: What constitutes success? How can we manage the many small failures that are required in order to discover the factors that will lead to long-term survival? How can we incorporate new information not just on the surface but deep in the "DNA" of our processes? How can we create systems that are robust and unique yet still open enough to allow for true exchange?

Natural Scorecard: U.S. Dollar Evolution

Exchange is at the heart of long-term evolution, and there are many forms of exchange that are employed in investing: there are stock exchanges, of course, but also exchanges of information, exchanges of wealth, and more human exchanges as well—those of connection and collaboration. One form of exchange, the use of modern currency, is so ubiquitous that we rarely stop to consider it in depth.

There are fascinating and important debates to be had regarding the U.S. dollar: some argue for the return of the gold standard or some other measure of value that is linked to tangible assets. Others are intensely focused on monetary policy or on links between the dollar, deficits, and debt. These are essential questions, to be sure, but for the purposes of this analysis, we want to narrow our examination to a simple and specific consideration of the dollar in one of its primary roles: as a means of exchange.

Think of this one main function of the dollar, **means of exchange,** and how it has evolved over time. A condensed view of the history of exchange includes a progression that looks something like this:

- Barter—direct exchange of services. "I'll milk your cow if you feed my pig."

- Barter—direct exchange of goods. "I'll trade you two pigs for your cow."
- Commodities as currency. "I'll give you a peck of salt for your cow, and then you can trade the peck of salt with that other guy for two pigs."
- Coins as currency. "Thank goodness we don't have to drag around kegs of salt anymore! Here's a sack of gold coins as payment for your cow instead."
- Paper currency. "Even better! Here's a promise of value in exchange for your cow."

As this evolution took place, several clear advantages emerged: for one thing, more and more people were able to connect with one another. By the time we were using commodities as currency, the cow owner did not need to know the pig owner in order for them to trade. And just as importantly, we could carry around salt (or coins or paper) instead of pulling a cart full of pigs behind us as a means of exchange. So we could trade over longer distances and longer time frames, as well as between more and more people.

This evolution of scope also involved a transfer of **trust**. Instead of having direct trust in the quality of the pig or the honesty of the owner, with currency as the means of exchange we could agree on a value, trusting in that currency instead of the people or products at hand. Curiously, as money infiltrated many parts of the economy that previously relied on direct ties, this circulation of trust was not one-way. People began to evolve their use of money, linking money to specific sorts of trusted social relationships by using it for indirect transactions like housekeeping allowances, pin money, gift certificates, tips, and food stamps.[7]

More recently, we have moved from using paper to electrons as our currency. It might seem like forever since you had to physically go to a bank to withdraw money, but this electronic evolution has really occurred just in the last thirty years—the blink of an eye in evolutionary terms. As these electronic forms of finance have accelerated, trust in financial institutions has eroded: finance is the least trusted industry globally, according to the Edelman Trust Barometer.[8] There are many plausible and obvious reasons for this erosion of trust in finance, of course, but part of the decline might have been enabled by our high trust in the dollar. When our trust in currency is high, perhaps our trust in institutions is somehow less essential.

Curiously, the latest evolution in currency, Bitcoin, includes a declaration of "non-trust" in its origin paper, declaring: "What is needed is an electronic payment system based on cryptographic proof instead of trust, allowing any two parties to transact with one another without the need for a trusted third party."[9] This evolution of trust with respect to currencies is a vital piece of the puzzle: Do we need currency that eliminates trust, or do we need currency where our trust is more justified than it might be today?

Trust is usually considered a human-centric quality, but its equivalent exists throughout natural systems. Most of what we would consider trust in nature is a result of effective **function** and proven mutualisms, and that includes the evolution of function over the longer term. When we take the longer view, a wider range of questions appears and a wider range of assumptions is revealed. We think of the dollar as if it's a static, permanent force, when in fact it has only existed in its current form for a couple of decades.

Given the rapid evolution of the dollar's functions, it's no wonder that lots of public attention is focused on those expanded functions and whether they are appropriate. Certainly, it is vital to question how and why we are using this particular economic organism in the ways that we are. But it's just as vital to place all of those questions into a much longer-term evolutionary context. For now, let's think about the central functions of the dollar, as a direct **means of exchange** and **store of value,** and how those functions hold up against the principles of effective evolution:

- **Does it replicate what works?** Yes, the dollar builds upon the features of earlier exchange mechanisms and continues to perform their essential functions.
- **Does it integrate the unexpected?** Pretty well—the dollar has taken on different and evolving roles, and has served as a means of exchange in different environments over time.
- **Does it reshuffle information?** The dollar has taken in lots of inputs over time, from changes in policy to changes in other surrounding currencies. This is not quite a direct parallel to biological pollination and reproduction, but the dollar has interfaced with lots of other currency organisms over time and has evolved to maintain its overall function throughout.

On this basis, the dollar looks pretty sound (no pun intended)—a solid B grade. However, it's not just a means of exchange anymore. How has the U.S. dollar evolved over the past century?

A quick survey of recent decades shows that we have evolved our use of the dollar to include all sorts of functions beyond being a (fairly) local means of exchange. Early on, function was extended to include acting as cross-border means of exchange and, more recently, as global means of exchange. Even more recently, the U.S. dollar has become a monetary policy tool, an international reserve currency, and a means of managing political as well as economic international relations.

Here is a brief summary of the extended functions of the U.S. dollar in recent decades:

- The dollar still serves its earlier function as a **means of exchange,** on a more and more extended basis.
- It also is used as a **means of intervention,** bought and sold by central banks and used as a tool in monetary policy; it was used in programs like the Marshall Plan and the Dodge Line to finance U.S. exports for rebuilding overseas after World War II.
- The dollar has increasingly been the default currency for global contracts, used as a **means of invoicing,** even for trade that has no other link to the United States.
- And it is used to determine exchange rates for other national currencies as well as many alternative currencies, making it a **means of pegging value** for these others.
- In addition to its role as a store of value, dollar-denominated assets are held by private agents, where the dollar is serving as a **means of banking and holding reserves.**[10]

Of crucial importance, as these extended functions were evolving for the dollar, its connection to other stores of value ended when the gold standard was eliminated in 1971. Since that time the dollar has performed broader and broader functions with a greater and greater reliance on trust. There is no longer a precious metal underpinning our currency's value, which may prove vital when trust wanes.

Given the cross-purposes noted above, let's examine this multifunctional view of the dollar's alignment with "evolve to survive":

- **Does it replicate what works?** Well, we've continued to use the dollar as an effective means of exchange, and in fact this use has broadened. But we have taken up other mechanisms' failures and put them all on the dollar, when we could have been evolving new and different tools instead. Ultimately, this overburdening may circle back to undermine the primary function of basic commerce as well.
- **Does it integrate the unexpected?** When any mechanism is expected to fulfill disparate functions, it's harder and harder to integrate the unexpected in one area without throwing others out of balance.
- **Does it reshuffle information?** Since there is only one national currency in the United States (and increasingly concentrated use globally), there is very little chance for cross-pollination, for the introduction of new features from the outside. This is a serious systemic risk.

Though natural systems do exhibit multifunctional design, perhaps we have discovered the limits of multifunctionality when it comes to our many uses for the U.S. dollar. The dollar as default currency may have made sense when the United States accounted for most of the industrial production in the global trading world. However, now the U.S. is only about 20 percent of trading output, yet the dollar is still our major global currency. This is a mismatch that seems unlikely to persist.[11] We have piled more and more requirements on this one form of currency, quashing opportunities for other forms and mechanisms to take on some of the functional burden.

Evolution: Local Currencies and Other Forms of Exchange

Though the dollar may be overburdened with our extended expectations, there are plenty of examples of alternate forms of exchange in the world. Lots of attention has been heaped on Bitcoin, but we are already using many forms of alternative, electronic currency without even thinking about it. That gift card from your grandma? Electronic currency. Airline miles? Electronic currency. Your frequent-drinker card that you swipe at the coffee shop? Electronic currency.[12]

One of the most interesting alternative currencies, though, is not enabled by the Internet or fancy cryptography: the WIR is over seventy-five years old. Launched in Zurich in the depths of the 1930s depression, the WIR is an organized bartering system—not for individuals, but for businesses.[13] Value is pegged to the Swiss franc, but WIR francs are not convertible, so there is incentive for them to circulate within the system. The WIR system is a small portion of Switzerland's economy, well under 1 percent of GDP, but it has been shown to provide disproportionate stabilization power, due to its countercyclicality.[14] In short, when other financial groups are retrenching, the WIR bank tends to be more active.

The motto of the WIR founders strikes a notably different chord than the Bitcoin manifesto: "Free exchange of goods and services, without exploitation of our fellowmen, and without government coercion."[15] An independent, trust-based system.

There are robust local currencies across the world, from Brazil to the Berkshires.[16] And, increasingly, there are other means of exchange for both goods and services, such as Freecycle and TaskRabbit. What is perhaps most encouraging is that newer technological platforms enable this sort of exchange on a scale that is both wide and deep. Businesses like Airbnb and Buzzcar allow the sharing economy to soar past the limits of physical proximity.

The rapid growth of these models has been enabled by several critical factors, notes Robin Chase, founder of Zipcar and now Buzzcar. First, there is tremendous excess capacity of stuff in certain circles, and tremendous need in others. Cars are one of the most obvious examples of this excess capacity, but power tools, spare bedrooms, and even free time all have similar capacity dynamics. Second, there is a network of peer collaborators: individuals who are active participants in the system, not just passive consumers. And third, there are technology platforms to facilitate all of the matchmaking, validation, and technical expertise that are needed. Skype, Wikipedia, YouTube: all of these models rely on easy-to-access platforms that enable excess capacity—from hardware to ideas—to be more effectively deployed.[17]

These new means of exchange embody evolution, incorporating change as it occurs. They allow room to incorporate small failures gracefully in order to improve the overall system. They are inherently open, transparent models, and trust is enabled through that transparency. In evolutionary terms, these developments are replicating what works while also integrating new features, functions, and capabilities.

Pathway to Practice

Our reliance on just one form of currency to fulfill so many functions has resulted in an inherently fragile, overburdened situation. Unless you happen to be the chair of the Federal Reserve, or maybe secretary of the Treasury, it's unlikely that major decisions about the fate of the U.S. dollar lie in your hands. Still, this example gives us some helpful guidance on how to approach our own investing.

First, we can check to see whether our intentions are embodied ones or whether they are just that, good intentions. Do your investments "walk the walk"? Whether you are aiming for steady dividend income, tangible community benefit, or responsible consumer choices, it's helpful to test our actions versus our hopes, even if we can't always fully assess the outcomes.

Second, we can clarify our vision of success, adding

creativity that goes beyond simple dollars or percentages. In evolutionary terms, success is usually defined as survival. What would success look like for your investing? A fancy new car? A college fund for your grandkids? A farm in your town that is saved from development? A longed-for trip taken or musical instrument mastered? How can we gently "mutate" and try new variations, recognizing that some won't work out the way we hope? How can we help to perpetuate the ones that are successful?

Finally, we can be alert to whether the systems we engage with are open or closed. When I hear "open systems," I often still hear a voice in my head that translates to "unsafe" or "not secure." I have the urge to lock something. But an open system is just that—open. It allows for iteration, for inputs from the outside, for healthy rejuvenation and incorporation of new elements. I think of the long-term history of the United States as one of the greatest illustrations of an open system: our country has thrived in large part due to constant immigration of new people, new ideas, and new endeavors.

Sowing Seeds of Evolution in Your Own Investing

As I translate this evolutionary approach to my own investing, I ask myself, how might this investment change over time? Is it flexible enough to evolve on its own or will I have to be the one to do the adjusting? A thirty-year T-bill, for example, is a closed system; its design predetermines structure and duration. That's great if it is a match for your needs, but investing with too much rigidity—whether in form, function, or philosophy—leaves us flat-footed when times change.

How can we think about long-term evolution for our investing?

- **Be clear on what constitutes success** for our investments.
- **Be wary of overloading any one type of investing with too much function.** Maybe all of our giving-related investing should not be writing checks to charities, for example. We can invest time. We can invest in responsible for-profit entities. We can invest in a more just world with our consumer dollars.
- **Allow for multiple "currencies"**—different forms of investing, different reasons for investing, different organizations for investing. Different whats, whys, and hows.
- **Invest with pollination in mind.** Pay attention to the openness of your investing over time. Closed systems appear to be consistent because they're rigid, but that is often false comfort when conditions change.

As we employ the principles of healthy evolution, we can ensure our own survival.

We can foster pollination and evolution through open systems.

We can shift from static to dynamic.

PART III

Cultivation and Care

Biomimicry Investing: Resilient, Regenerative, Reconnected

It is easy to dodge our responsibilities, but we cannot dodge the consequences of dodging our responsibilities.[1]
—Josiah Charles Stamp

This book has explored a number of detailed examples from the financial world, presenting a long list of challenges. When I step back from the detail, though, I see just three main fissures that run straight through to the bedrock of our systems. Repairing these three will bring us back toward the true nature of investing, toward a connected, beneficial financial ecosystem that is in service to our communities and our planet.

First, we have disconnected investing from the real world. Automating analysis and trading, outsourcing expertise, and adding layers of synthesis and complication have improved efficiencies and created certain new opportunities. But most of these efficiencies are of the shallow sort, focused only on speed and immediate cost. And most of those opportunities have proven to be fleeting, looming large in the short term but fading quickly into losses over the longer term. **Reconnecting**, in all of its forms, is the first task of an engaged investor.

Second, we have narrowed our perspectives in a false and needless way. We think of investing as only what shows on our brokerage statements, when in reality we are investing with every action, every decision, every dollar. We consider profit and cost to be only what's shown on financial statements, forgetting that we ourselves invented accounting. Those numbers are tools, not truth. We examine data every day, every second, every microsecond, just because we can, pulling our attention away from the months and years to come, shrinking our field of vision to exclude the most important consequences and most complete views of investment returns. This shrunken focus traps us in a mindset of extraction. Broadening our definitions to include longer term and more multidimensional measures of profit, cost, and investing is the first step to creating a **regenerative** system, not just for finance but for our entire society and our entire planet.

Finally, we have chosen to create complicated, rigid structures, instead of flexible, adaptive ones. Like the little pigs, afraid of the big bad wolf, we have built more and more defenses against the threats of our world, both real and imagined. But what happens when the threat of a big wind is replaced by a flood? We can never build complete defenses against uncertainty. And yet from investment allocation boxes to complicated regulations to entire firms based on structured investment products, we have chosen the false security of ever-increasing structure, all the while increasing our ultimate fragility. Appreciating the need for adaptation, over all time frames, throughout all circumstances, and at every level of scale is the beginning of creating a more **resilient** system.

Fortunately, there is plenty of cause for optimism. I must admit, as I dug into the investing examples of ventures gone awry, I was afraid that I'd find a core that was rotten, a system that was entirely lost to anyone seeking to reclaim the true nature of investing. I found just the opposite: time and time again, the kernel of true service, true need, true exchange, and true profit was alive and well. Admittedly, it was sometimes so small or covered up or removed from its original state that it was hard to identify, but still, it was there. At the core, if we peel off enough layers, there is still something solid to be built upon.

Also, we are surrounded by abundance. We have tools and capabilities for sharing knowledge and wisdom that have never existed before. We have the ability to connect not just in superficial ways but in deep and lasting ways across great spans of time and space and culture. We have growing understanding—both technically and emotionally. We have not just tangible resources but also far more important gifts to draw upon: the wisdom of nature as mentor, model, measure, and muse.

Finally, we have ourselves! Throughout this book, I've emphasized that humans are a part of nature, and this is a delightful, vital truth. We also are pretty amazing and unique creatures. We have morals and ethics and the capacity for complex thought. We have tremendous capabilities that demand an equivalent level of responsibility and stewardship and engagement and care. We have compassion and empathy along with information and skill. We have the ability to choose to cooperate for the greater good.

With all of these resources, we can engage in a rebirth of creative, independent investment thinking. We can take up our true and full responsibilities—to ourselves, to each other, to our home. We can unbox our decision making. We can reweave our loose threads of investing back into the fabric of the world.

Using nature as the ultimate investing framework isn't romantic; it's right. The narrowed, rigid approach we've taken served a purpose in its time, but it was a small purpose and a small window of time. This falsely linear view is an intellectually lazy one, unprofitable, and not even very interesting. With all of our resources, all of our gifts, we can do better. We have a responsibility to do better. And here is the greatest secret of all: embracing that messy multidimensional complexity is so much more rewarding. It's even more fun.

Here are the transformations needed, the steps on our path toward reclaiming the true nature of investing:

- From efficient to effective
- From synthetic to simplified
- From maximized to optimized
- From disconnected to reconnected
- From mechanical to mindful
- From static to dynamic

When we put them all together, we move our entire system:

- From fragile to resilient
- From extractive to regenerative
- From disconnected to reconnected

This is a system that's worthy of our full engagement, our full attention, our full participation, and it is ours to create, with nature as our most valued guide. This is what "fully invested" really means. This is the true Nature of Investing.

I would like to beg you . . . to try to love the questions themselves as if they were locked rooms or books written in a very foreign language. Don't search for the answers, which could not be given to you now, because you would not be able to live them. And the point is to live everything. Live the questions now. Perhaps then, someday far in the future, you will gradually, without even noticing it, live your way into the answer.

—Rainer Maria Rilke

Timshel: The Power of Choice[1]

Thinking is the talking of the soul with itself.[2]
—PLATO

Throughout this book, one call has sounded time and time again: the call to think. Independent, creative engaged thought, when paired with constructive action, is one of our most powerful gifts. Timshel, the title of this chapter, is inspired by John Steinbeck's *East of Eden*, where the word's meaning is debated. In scripture, "timshel" is part of the verses on Cain and Abel; sometimes it is translated as "thou shalt" (a proclamation), while other times it translates as "do thou" (a commandment). What the character Lee in *East of Eden* discovers is a third possibility, one that he deems the most accurate: "thou mayest." Free will. Choice.

To unite thought and action, though, requires two conditions. First, our definitions of thought and action need to be encompassing, with room for emotion and intuition and spirit, too. Second, our underlying values and our guiding principles need to be crystal clear—just like the honeybees when they're seeking a new home. Here, then, are my own beliefs.

I believe

...that "and" is better than "or."

...that bridges are better than boxes.

...that the natural world offers insights more powerful than those our imaginations could ever create.

...that the systems we create do exactly what we designed them to do—and that therefore we have the power to change them to do different, better things.

...that stories are important. They connect us, inspire us, and make the abstract real.

...that needless fear drives most of the problems of the world, and necessary fear drives the rest.

...that most people, most of the time, want to "bend toward justice."

...that extending our time horizon and expanding our focus makes it easier to see true cost and true profit, which naturally leads to more optimized investment decisions.

...that investment, in its truest and broadest sense, is a tremendous force for positive change.

These are my beliefs; they don't have to be yours. But investing our precious resources—time, energy, talents, wealth—is an act worthy of deep reflection and consideration. **Investing is not just a practical necessity; it is embodied belief.** This endeavor is worthy of our full attention, and it is well served by embracing the full spectrum of the world's wisdom—natural, spiritual, emotional, and intellectual. This bank of wisdom is our truest capital, our deepest well, offering endless possibilities for investing in the world that we want to see.

Here we are, on this earth, our home. Together.
Surrounded by wisdom and power and potential.
Shhhhh.
Look. Listen.

Welcome home.

Notes

Saved By the Bee

1 Thomas D Seeley, *Honeybee Democracy* (Princeton, NJ: Princeton University Press, 2010). See also http://www.cornell.edu/video/honeybee-democracy-book-talk-by-thomas-seeley.

The Roots of Biomimicry Investing

1 Immanuel Kant, *Critique of Practical Reason* (Mineola, NY: Dover Publications, Inc. 2004 reprint of 1909 publication by Longmans, Green, and Co. (New York).

2 Dayna Baumeister, *Biomimicry Resource Handbook: A Seed Bank of Best Practices* (Missoula, MT: Biomimicry 3.8, 2013). See also http://blog.interface.com/category/biomimicry-8.

3 Iris Marion Young, "Responsibility and Global Labor Justice," *Journal of Political Philosophy* 12, no. 4 (2004): 365–388.

4 Major resources for biomimicry include: Dayna Baumeister, *Biomimicry Resource Handbook: A Seed Bank of Best Practices* (Missoula, MT: Biomimicry 3.8, 2013); Janine Benyus, *Biomimicry: Innovation Inspired by Nature* (New York: William Morrow, 1997).

5 Hazel Henderson and Janine Benyus, "Statement on Transforming Finance Based on Ethics and Life's Principles," 2012, http://www.ethicalmarkets.com/statement-on-transforming-finance-based-on-ethics-and-lifes-principles.

NOTES

Transformation 1: From Efficient to Effective

1 D.B. Cater and N.R. Lawrie, "Some Histochemical and Biochemical Observations on the Preen Gland," *The Journal of Physiology III* (1950): 23l–243; D. McFarland, *A Dictionary of Animal Behaviour* (New York: Oxford Press, 2006), 163.

2 G.J. Tattersall, D.V. Andrade, and A.S. Abe, "Heat Exchange from the Toucan Bill Reveals a Controllable Vascular Thermal Radiator," *Science* 325: 5939 (2009): 468–470.

3 Elena Tricarico and Francesca Gherardi, "Resource Assessment in Hermit Crabs: The Worth of Their Own Shell," *Behavioral Ecology* 18, no. 3 (2007): 615–620.

4 Yoseph Bar-Cohen, *Biomimetics: Biologically Inspired Technologies* (Boca Raton, FL: CRC/Taylor & Francis, 2006). Cited by: http://www.asknature.org/strategy/2765a76a09f7cdbf84c79 72ed539a252.

5 Jack Welch, "Eating and Dreaming," post for *Linked In*, July 25, 2013, http://www.linkedin.com/today/post/article/20130725154204-86541065-eating-and-dreaming.

6 *Good Will Hunting*, 1997, Gus Van Sant, director.

7 Investment Company Institute, *2013 Investment Company Fact Book*, 53rd edition (2013), 79–80.

8 Christopher Phillips with Francis Kinniry Jr. and Todd Schlanger, "The Case for Index-Fund Investing," *Vanguard*, April 2013. Fund performance data from Morningstar, https://personal.vanguard.com/pdf/s296.pdf.

9 Warren Buffett, "Letter to Shareholders," *Berkshire Hathaway Annual Report*, 2005. http://www.berkshirehathaway.com/2005ar/2005ar.pdf.

10 Andrew Ross Sorkin, "Doubts Raised on Value of Investment Consultants to Pensions," *The New York Times*, September 30, 2013.

11 Investment Company Institute, *2013 Investment Company Fact Book*, 53rd edition (2013), 79–80.

12 Josh Charlson, et al. "Target-Date Series Research Paper: 2013 Survey," http://corporate.morningstar.com/us/documents/ResearchPapers/2013TargetDate.pdf.

13 PriceMetrix, *The State of Retail Wealth Management: Third Annual Report* (February 2013), http://www.pricemetrix.com/cms/wp-content/uploads/PriceMetrix-Insights_The-State-of-Retail-Wealth-Management-2012_English.pdf.

14 There is a deep literature on this subject in behavioral finance and financial literacy research, including this meta-analysis: Daniel Fernandes, John Lynch, and Richard Netemeyer, "Financial Education and Downstream Financial Behaviors," forthcoming in *Management Science* (October 8, 2013). See also http://www.nytimes.com/2013/10/06/business/financial-literacy-beyond-the-classroom.html?pagewanted=all&_r=0.

15 Gokce Sargut and Rita Gunther McGrath, "Learning to Live with Complexity," *Harvard Business Review*, September 1, 2011. See also www.santafe.edu.

Transformation 2: From Synthetic to Simple

1 John Pickrell, "Peacock Plumage Secrets Uncovered," National Geographic News, October 17, 2003; *Scientific American* 306 (2012), 74–79, published online: 17 April 2012 | doi:10.1038/scientificamerican0512-74. Also: Philip Ball, "Nature's Color Tricks," *Scientific American* 306, no. 5, May 2012, 74–79.

2 Tree of Life website: tolweb.org/Diatoms/21810, A. Scheffel, N. Poulsen, S. Shian, N. Kroger, "Nanopatterned Protein Microrings from a Diatom That Direct Silica Morphogenesis," PNAS 108, no. 8 (2011): 3175–3180, http://AskNature.org.

3 H.A. Harper, V.W. Rodwell, and P.A. Mayes, *Review of Physiological Chemistry*, 16th ed. (Los Altos, California: Lange Medical Publications, 1977), via howthingswork.com.

4 "The Landmarks of Snake-Poison Literature," https://play.google.com/store/books/details?id=aeoyAQAAMAAJ&rdid=book-aeoyAQAAMAAJ&rdot=1, and "Snake Venom Is Being Used To Cure, Rather Than Kill," http://www.economist.com/news/science-and-technology/21569015-snake-venom-being-used-cure-rather-kill-toxic-medicine.

5 Janine Benyus, *Biomimicry: Innovation Inspired by Nature* (New York: William Morrow, 1997), 7.

6 David Robertson and Bill Breen, *Brick by Brick: How LEGO Rewrote the Rules of Innovation and Conquered the Global Toy Industry* (New York: Random House, 2013), **[Au: page number(s)?].**

7 *It's a Wonderful Life*, 1946, Frank Capra, director.

8 Elena Loutskina,"The Role of Securitization in Bank Liquidity and Funding Management," draft, 2010.

9 Official Report, Government Printing Office, "The Financial Crisis Inquiry Report: Final Report of the National Commission on the Causes of the Financial and Economic Crisis in the United States." Washington, D.C.: U.S. Government Printing Office. January, 2011, 70.

10 Thompson Reuters, "Debt Capital Markets Review: Managing Underwriters," first quarter 2013.

11 Synthetics have an added wrinkle in that they are zero-sum: for this structure to be created, every investor making a positive bet requires another investor to make an equivalent negative bet. This led to numerous moral and ethical questions for securities creators, as motivations for appropriate disclosure and responsibility were often at odds with profitability. These transactions are also private and thus unregulated, so it's hard to find accurate aggregate data. But just one firm, Goldman Sachs, packaged and sold synthetic CDO's with face value of $66 billion in the three years ended May 2007. Official Report—Government Printing Office. "The Financial Crisis Inquiry Report: Final Report of the National Commission on the Causes of the Financial and Economic Crisis in the United States." Washington, D.C.: U.S. Government Printing Office. January, 2011, 70.

12 See greenamerica.org or breakupwithyourmegabank.org.

13 "Credit Union Earnings Hit All-Time High," March 1, 2013, http://www.ncua.gov/News/Pages/NW20130301CUEarnings.aspx.

NOTES

Transformation 3: From Maximized to Optimized

1 William M. Kier and Andrew M. Smith, "The Structure and Adhesive Mechanism of Octopus Suckers," *Integrative and Comparative Biology* 42, no. 6 (2002):1146–1153, http://dx.doi.org/10.1093/icb/42.6.1146.

2 Laurent Keller and Elizabeth Gordon, *The Lives of Ants* (New York: Oxford University Press, 2009), chapters 9 and 10.

3 "Declining US High Frequency Trading," *The New York Times*, October, 15, 2012. Data source: TABB Group, http://www.nytimes.com/interactive/2012/10/15/business/Declining-US-High-Frequency-Trading.html?ref=business.

4 There are many versions of these depictions; look for "flash crash trading video" and dozens of different representations appear.

5 US CFTC and SEC, "Findings Regarding the Market Events of May 6, 2010: Report of the Staffs of the CFTC and SEC to the Join Advisory Committee on Emerging Regulatory Issues," September 30, 2010, http://www.sec.gov/news/studies/2010/marketevents-report.pdf.

6 Dan Barnes, "NYSE Flash Crash Reignites the Circuit Breaker Debate," *Financial News*, June 26, 2013, http://www.efinancialnews.com/story/2013-06-26/nyse-flash-crash-reignites-circuit-breaker-debate?ea9c8a2de0ee111045601ab04d673622.

7 Alexis C. Madrigal, "No Easy Tech Explanation for What Caused Wall St. 'Flash Crash,'" *The Atlantic*, July 14, 2010, http://www.theatlantic.com/technology/archive/2010/07/no-easy-tech-explanation-for-what-caused-wall-st-flash-crash/59766/.

8 US CFTC and SEC, "Findings Regarding the Market Events of May 6, 2010: Report of the Staffs of the CFTC and SEC to the Join Advisory Committee on Emerging Regulatory Issues," September 30, 2010, 6, http://www.sec.gov/news/studies/2010/marketevents-report.pdf.

9 Justin Fox, "The Economics of Well-Being," *Harvard Business Review*, January–February 2012, http://hbr.org/2012/01/the-economics-of-well-being/ar/.

10 Robert F. Kennedy, remarks at the University of Kansas, March 18, 1968, transcript from the John F. Kennedy Presidential Library and Museum, http://www.jfklibrary.org/Research/Research-Aids/Ready-Reference/RFK-Speeches/Remarks-of-Robert-F-Kennedy-at-the-University-of-Kansas-March-18-1968.aspx

11 Judy Wicks, *Good Morning, Beautiful Business: The Unexpected Journey of an Activist Entrepreneur and Local-Economy Pioneer* (White River Junction, VT: Chelsea Green Publishing, 2013), 157.

12 B-corporation, "Declaration of Interdependence," Accessed August 2013. http://www.bcorporation.net/what-are-b-corps/the-b-corp-declaration.

Transformation 4: From Disconnected to Reconnected

1 P. Gorzelak, J. Stolarski, P. Dubois, C. Kopp, and A. Meibom, "26Mg Labeling of the Sea Urchin Regenerating Spine: Insights into Echinoderm Biomineralization Process," *Journal of Structural Biology*, 176 (2011): 119–126, via AskNature.org.

2 John Roach, "No Nemo: Anemones, Not Parents, Protect Clownfish," National Geographic News. Accessed August 27, 2007, via AskNature.org; also J.T. Szczebak, R.P. Henry, F.A. Al-Horani, and N.E. Chadwick, "Anemonefish Oxygenate Their Anemone Hosts at Night," *The Journal of Experimental Biology* 216 (2013), 970–976.

3 Thomas Nørgaard and Marie Dacke, "Fog-Basking Behaviour and Water Collection Efficiency in Namib Desert Darkling Beetles," *Frontiers in Zoology* 7:23 (2010). Also M.K. Seely, C.J. Lewis, K.A. O'Brien, and A.E. Suttle, "Fog Response of Tenebrionid Beetles in the Namib Desert," *Journal of Arid Environments* 6:2 (1983): 135–143, via AskNature.org.

4 A. Thornton and K. McAuliffe, *Science* 313, no. 5784 (July 14, 2006): 227–229.

5 General Electric company website, Investor Relations section, http://www.ge.com/investor-relations.

6 Felix Liechti and others, "First Evidence of a 200-Day Non-stop Flight in a Bird," *Nature Communications* 4, article 2554

(October 8, 2013). Cited by *Smithsonian Magazine*, http://blogs.smithsonianmag.com/science/2013/10/this-bird-can-stay-in-flight-for-six-months-straight/?utm_source=smithsoniantopic&utm_medium=email&utm_campaign=20131013-Weekender.

7 Shefali Sharma and Steve Suppan, "Commodity Market Deregulation and Food Prices," Institute for Agriculture and Trade Policy Presentation at UNCATD Symposium, June 22, 2011, http://www.iatp.org/files/Commodity market deregulation and food prices.pdf.

8 Rick Schmitt, "Prophet and Loss," *Stanford Magazine*, March/April 2009, http://alumni.stanford.edu/get/page/magazine/article/?article_id=30885.

9 Commodity index fund data from Oliver DeShutter, "Food Commodities Speculation and Food Price Crises," UN Special Rapporteur on the Right to Food, September, 2010; much of this timeline is abstracted from Ann Berg, "Commodity Funds in Retreat?" special feature in FAO *Food Outlook*, June 2013: 66-68; Frederick Kaufman, "The Food Bubble: How Wall Street Starved Millions and Got Away with It," *Harper's Magazine*, June 2010, 27–34.

10 Shefali Sharma and Steve Suppan, "Commodity Market Deregulation and Food Prices," Institute for Agriculture and Trade Policy Presentation at UNCATD Symposium, June 22, 2011, http://www.iatp.org/files/Commodity market deregulation and food prices.pdf.

11 Frederick Kaufman, "The Food Bubble: How Wall Street Starved Millions and Got Away with It," *Harper's Magazine*, June 2010, 34.

12 M. Lagi, K. Z. Bertrand, and Y. Bar-Yam, "Food Crises: A Quantitative Model of Food Prices Including Speculators and Ethanol Conversion," September 21, 2011, http://necsi.edu/research/social/food_prices.pdf.

13 Michael Pollan, "What's Eating America?" *Smithsonian*, June 15, 2006. Also: *The Omnivore's Dilemma: A Natural History of Four Meals* (New York: Penguin Books, 2007).

14 M. Lagi, K.Z. Bertrand, and Y. Bar-Yam, "The Food Crises and Political Instability in North Africa and the Middle East,"

arXiv:1108.2455, August 10, 2011, http://necsi.edu/research/social/food_crises.pdf.

15 "The Price of Protest, So Far," graphic from *The Economist*, July 14, 2011, http://www.economist.com/blogs/dailychart/2011/07/arab-spring-death-toll.

16 John Fullerton, "Commodities Are Different," Capital Institute post, August 5, 2013, http://capitalinstitute.org/blog/commodities-are-different-"full-world"-part-3 - .UjNYDaXIhwY.

17 Slow Money website: http://slowmoney.org.

18 BALLE website: http://bealocalist.org.

19 Michael Swack, Jack Northrup, and Eric Hangen, "CDFI Industry Analysis Summary Report," Carsey Institute, Spring 2012.

Transformation 5: From Mechanical to Mindful

1 Jennifer S. Holland, "Living Color," *National Geographic*, June 2008, http://ngm.nationalgeographic.com/2008/06/nudibranchs/holland-text; Terry Gosliner, "Nudibranchs, Corals, and Readers' Questions," *The New York Times*, Scientist at Work, August 10, 2010, http://scientistatwork.blogs.nytimes.com/2010/08/10/nudibranchs-corals-and-readers-questions.

2 Referenced in Alice Schroeder, *The Snowball: Warren Buffett and the Business of Life* (New York: Bantam Dell, 2008), 201.

3 Leslie Christian, former CEO of Portfolio 21, has developed a framework for portfolio theory to evolve in a way that is more complete and helpful. See Leslie Christian, "A New Foundation for Portfolio Management," RSF Social Finance and Portfolio 21, 2011, http://rsfsocialfinance.org/wp-content/uploads/downloads/2011/10/A-New-Foundation-for-Portfolio-Management.pdf.

4 Will Danoff, in conversation, sometime around 1990–1991.

5 ICI Factbook, 2013, "Number of Funds in the Mutual Fund Industry," 146. There were over 8000 mutual funds by the year 2000.

6 Don Phillips and Paul Kaplan (Morningstar employees), "The Morningstar Approach to Mutual Fund Analysis—Part II," in *Mutual Funds: Portfolio Structures, Analysis, Management,*

and Stewardship (Hoboken, New Jersey: John Wiley & Sons, Inc., 2010), 177–178.

7 Diana Del Guercio and Paula Tkac, "Star Power: The Effect of Morningstar Ratings on Mutual Fund Flows," November 2003, http://wwwdocs.fce.unsw.edu.au/banking/seminar/2004/Diane%20Del%20Guercio.pdf. Note that this study examined the effect of Morningstar's "star" ratings, not their categorization tool, but the two are intermingled in many publications and, it seems, in the minds of many investors.

8 ICI Factbook 2013, "Target Date and Lifestyle Mutual Funds," 194.

9 Frank H. Knight, *Risk, Uncertainty, and Profit* (Boston: Houghton and Mifflin, 1921) Chapter 1; Michael J. Mauboussin, "Interdisciplinary Perspectives on Risk," CAS) Mauboussin on Strategy, Legg Mason Capital Management, August 15, 2006; Also: Michael J. Mauboussin, Think Twice (Boston: Harvard Business Press, 2009).). See: http://www.econlib.org/library/Knight/knRUP.html.

10 www.transitionus.org

Transformation 6: From Static to Dynamic

1 This quote is attributed to John Maynard Keynes, but an original source has not been verified.

2 Brian Switek, "In Evolution's Race, Horseshoe Crabs Took a Slower Pace," *Wired*, November 22, 2011. With reference to: R. Feldman, et al (2011), "Remarkable Preservation of a New Genus and Species of Limuline Horseshoe Crab from the Cretaceous of Texas, USA," *Palaeontology* 54:6, November 15, 2011, 1337–1346, DOI: 10.1111/j.1475-4983.2011.01103.x; Also: Huxley, T.H. 1877; Also: D. Prothero, Evolution: *What the Fossils Say and Why It Matters* (New York: Columbia University Press, 2007) 189–191.

3 L. Scott Mills and others, "Camouflage Mismatch in Seasonal Coat Color Due to Decreased Snow Duration," proceedings of the National Academy of Sciences of the United States of America 110, no. 18, http://www.pnas.org/content/110/18/7360.

4 "Mammoth Genome Project," Pennsylvania State University, http://mammoth.psu.edu/howCloseElephantMammoth.html.

5 Peter Lynch, *Beating the Street* (New York: Simon and Schuster, 1993), 117.

6 Jeremy Grantham, "My Sister's Pension Assets and Agency Problems," April 2012, published on gmo.com.

7 Viviana Zelizer, "Pasts and Futures of Economic Sociology," *American Behavioral Scientist* (2007) 1061, referencing her earlier work, *The Social Meaning of Money* (Princeton, NY: Princeton University Press, 1997).

8 Edelman Trust Barometer, 2013, http://www.edelman.com/insights/intellectual-property/trust-2013/trust-across-sectors/trust-in-financial-services.

9 Satoshi Nakamoto, "Bitcoin: A Peer-to-Peer Electronic Cash System," October 31, 2008, http://bitcoin.org/bitcoin.pdf.

10 This summary is largely based on Paul Krugman, "The International Role of the Dollar: Theory and Prospect," National Bureau of Economic Research, 1984: Exchange Rate Theory and Practice, 263-264, http://nber.org/chapters/c6838.pdf. Krugman's description in turn is largely based on the work of B.J. Cohen, *The Future of Sterling as an International Currency* (London: Macmillan, 1971).

11 Barry Eichengreen, "Managing a Multiple Reserve Currency World," *Insight*, Volume 8, November 10, 2010.

12 This commentary builds on some elements of Paul Kemp Robertson's TED Talk on Bitcoin. http://www.ted.com/talks/paul_kemp_robertson_bitcoin_sweat_tide_meet_the_future_of_branded_currency.html?source=facebook#.UfZqbzVjjSt.facebook.

13 Matthew Allen, "Cash Substitute Greases Business Wheels," Swiss Broadcasting Corporation, October 21, 2009, http://www.swissinfo.ch/eng/business/Cash_substitute_greases_business_wheels.html?cid=7613810.

14 James Stodder, "Complementary Credit Networks and Macro-Economic Stability: Switzerland's Wirtschaftsring," June 5, 2009. Appearing in Journal of Economic Behavior &

Organization, 72, October, 2009, 79–95, http://ewp.rpi.edu/hartford/~stoddj/BE/WIR_Update.pdf.

15 Erick Hansch, "Research for the International Independence Institute, 1972," notes via the Schumacher Library, via the New Economics Institute, http://neweconomy.net/publications/initial-results-wir-research-switzerland.

16 See this list via the Schumacher Center for a New Economics: http://centerforneweconomics.org/content/active-local-currencies.

17 Robin Chase, SXSW Eco Keynote Address, October 2013, http://sxsw.com/music-film-interactive-sxsw-eco/news/2013/watch-sxsw-eco-2013-robin-chase-keynote.

Biomimicry Investing: Resilient, Regenerative, Reconnected

1 Josiah Stamp, *Some Economic Factors in Modern Life* (London: P.S. King & Son, 1929).

Timshel: The Power of Choice

1 John Steinbeck, *East of Eden* (New York: Penguin Books, 1952).

2 Plato, Henry Cary, George Burges, and Henry Davis. *The Works of Plato*, Volume 6 (London: George Bell and Sons, 1902), 247.

Resources

I am thankful for the many resources that contributed to the development of this book, whether directly or indirectly. Below are just a few inspirations in the areas of natural science, investing and economy, and systems thinking.

Natural Science

Baumeister, Dayna. *Biomimicry Resource Handbook: A Seed Bank of Best Practices*. Missoula, MT: Biomimicry 3.8, 2013.

Benyus, Janine. *Biomimicry: Innovation Inspired by Nature*. New York: William Morrow, 1997.

Berry, Wendell. *The Unsettling of America*. San Francisco, CA: Sierra Club, 1996.

Jackson, Wes. *Consulting the Genius of the Place*. Berkeley, CA: Counterpoint, 2010.

Jackson, Wes. *Nature as Measure: The Selected Essays of Wes Jackson*. Berkeley, CA: Counterpoint, 2011.

Keller, Laurent, and Elizabeth Gordon. *The Lives of Ants*. New York: Oxford University Press, 2009.

McFarland, D. *A Dictionary of Animal Behaviour*. New York: Oxford Press, 2006.

McKibben, Bill. *Eaarth*. New York: Times Books, 2010.

Pollan, Michael. *The Omnivore's Dilemma: A Natural History of Four Meals*. New York: Penguin Books, 2007.

Seeley, Thomas D. *Honeybee Democracy*. Princeton, NJ: Princeton University Press, 2010.

Seeley, Thomas D. *The Wisdom of the Hive*. Cambridge, MA: Harvard University Press, 1996.

Stamets, Paul. *Mycelium Running*. Berkeley, CA: Ten Speed Press, 2005.

Tautz, Jurgen. *The Buzz About Bees: Biology of a Superorganism*. Berlin: Springer Verlag, 2008.

Wilson, E.O. *Biophilia*. Cambridge, MA: Harvard University Press, 1984.

Wilson, E.O. *Consilience: The Unity of Knowledge*. New York: Knopf, 1998.

Wilson, E.O., and Bert Hölldobler. *The Superorganism*. New York: W.W.Norton & Company, 2009.

Philosophy, Economy, Business, Investing, and Finance

Aburdene, Patricia. *Conscious Money*. New York: Atria Paperback, 2012.

Bishop, Matthew, and Michael Green. *Philanthrocapitalism: How the Rich Can Save the World*. New York: Bloomsbury Press, 2008 (U.S. subtitle: *How Giving Can Save the World*).

Buffett, Warren. *Berkshire Hathaway Letters to Shareholders, 1965–2012*. Max Olsen, ed.

Bugg-Levine, Antony, and Jed Emerson. *Impact Investing*. San Francisco, CA: Jossey-Bass, 2011.

Cortese, Amy. *Locavesting: The Revolution in Local Investing and How to Profit from It*. Hoboken, NJ: John Wiley & Sons, 2011.

Cottle, Sidney, with Roger Murray and Frank Block. *Graham and Dodd's Security Analysis, Fifth Edition*. New York: McGraw Hill, 1988.

Eisenstein, Charles. *Sacred Economics*. Berkeley, CA: North Atlantic, 2011.

Gansky, Lisa. *The Mesh*. New York: Penguin, 2010.

Graeber, David. *Debt: The First 5,000 Years*. New York: Melville House, 2011.

Graham, Benjamin, with Jason Zweig and Warren Buffett. *The Intelligent Investor.* New York: HarperCollins, 2009.

Henderson, Hazel, and Simran Sethi. *Ethical Markets: Growing the Green Economy.* Chelsea Green Publishing, 2007.

Henderson, Hazel, and Janine Benyus. "Statement on Transforming Finance Based on Ethics and Life's Principles." 2012. http://www.ethicalmarkets.com/statement-on-transforming-finance-based-on-ethics-and-lifes-principles/.

Kelly, Marjorie. *Owning Our Future.* San Francisco, CA: Berrett-Keller, 2012.

Lynch, Peter. *Beating the Street.* New York: Simon and Schuster, 1993.

Lynch, Peter. *One Up on Wall Street.* New York: Simon and Schuster, 1989.

Mauboussin, Michael J. *The Success Equation: Untangling Skill and Luck in Business, Sports, and Investing.* Boston: Harvard Business Press, 2012.

Mauboussin, Michael J. *Think Twice.* Boston: Harvard Business Press, 2009.

McKibben, Bill. *Deep Economy.* New York: Times Books, 2010

Munger, Charles T. *Poor Charlie's Almanack.* Marceline, MO: Walsworth Publishing Company, 2006.

Paulson, Henry M. Jr. *On the Brink.* New York: Hachette Group, 2010.

Rifkin, Jeremy. *The Third Industrial Revolution.* New York: Palgrave Macmillan, 2011.

Schroeder, Alice. *The Snowball: Warren Buffett and the Business of Life.* New York: Bantam Dell, 2008.

Schumacher, E.F. *Small Is Beautiful.* London: Blond and Briggs, 1973.

Sen, Amartya. *On Ethics and Economics.* Malden, MA: Blackwell, 1988.

Sorkin, Andrew Ross. *Too Big To Fail.* New York: Penguin Books, 2010.

Stiglitz, Joseph E., with Amartya Sen and Jean-Paul Fitoussi. *Mismeasuring Our Lives: Why GDP Doesn't Add Up.* New York: The New Press, 2010.

Tasch, Woody. *Inquiries into the Nature of Slow Money: Investing as if Food, Farms, and Fertility Mattered.* White River Junction, VT: Chelsea Green Publishing, 2008.

Twist, Lynne, and Teresa Barker. *The Soul of Money.* New York: W.W. Norton & Company, 2003.

Wicks, Judy. *Good Morning, Beautiful Business: The Unexpected Journey of an Activist Entrepreneur and Local-Economy Pioneer.* White River Junction, VT: Chelsea Green Publishing, 2013.

Behavioral Science, Systems Thinking, and Complex Adaptive Systems

Ariely, Dan. *Predictably Irrational.* New York: HarperCollins, 2009.

Bar-Yam, Yaneer. *Dynamics of Complex Systems.* New York: Perseus Books, 1997.

Bar-Yam, Yaneer. *Making Things Work: Solving Complex Problems in a Complex World.* Cambridge, MA: Knowledge Press, 2004.

Bowles, Samuel, and Herbert Gintis. *A Cooperative Species: Human Reciprocity and Its Evolution.* Princeton, NJ: Princeton University Press, 2011.

Gell-Mann, Murray. *The Quark and the Jaguar: Adventures in the Simple and the Complex.* New York: W.H. Freeman, 1994.

Kahneman, Daniel. *Thinking, Fast and Slow.* New York: Farrar, Strauss, and Giroux, 2011.

Mandelbrot, Benoit, and Richard L. Hudson. *The Misbehavior of Markets.* New York: Basic Books, 2004.

Meadows, Donella H. "Leverage Points: Places to Intervene in a System." *The Sustainability Institute*, 1999.

Meadows, Donnella H., and others. *The Limits to Growth.* New York: Universe Books, 1972.

Meadows, Donella H. *Thinking in Systems: A Primer.* White River Junction, VT: Chelsea Green Publishing Company, 2008.

Mitchell, Melanie. *Complexity: A Guided Tour.* New York: Oxford University Press, 2009.

Page, Scott. *The Difference.* Princeton, NJ: Princeton University Press, 2007.

Rifkin, Jeremy. *The Empathetic Civilization.* New York: Penguin, 2009.

Sandel, Michael. *Justice.* New York: Farrar, Straus and Giroux. 2009.

Sandel, Michael. *What Money Can't Buy.* New York: Farrar, Straus and Giroux, 2012.

Taleb, Nassim. *Antifragile: Things That Gain from Disorder.* New York: Random House, 2012.

Taleb, Nassim. *The Black Swan.* New York: Random House, 2007.

Zolli, Andrew, and Ann Marie Healy. *Resilience: Why Things Bounce Back.* New York: Simon and Schuster, 2012.

Zweig, Jason. *Your Money and Your Brain.* New York: Simon & Schuster, 2007.

References

Allen, Matthew. "Cash Substitute Greases Business Wheels." *Swiss Broadcasting Corporation*, October 21, 2009. http://www.swissinfo.ch/eng/business/Cash_substitute_greases_business_wheels.html?cid=7613810.

B-corporation. "Declaration of Interdependence." http://www.bcorporation.net/what-are-b-corps/the-b-corp-declaration.

Ball, Philip. "Nature's Color Tricks." *Scientific American* 306, 74-79 (2012). See also: 17 April 2012. doi:10.1038/scientificamerican0512-74.

BALLE website. http://bealocalist.org.

Bar-Cohen, Yoseph. *Biomimetics: Biologically Inspired Technologies.* Boca Raton, FL: CRC/Taylor & Francis, 2006. Cited by: http://www.asknature.org/strategy/2765a76a09f7cdbf84c7972ed539a252.

Barnes, Dan. "NYSE Flash Crash Reignites the Circuit Breaker Debate." *Financial News*, June 26, 2013. http://www.efinancialnews.com/story/2013-06-26/nyse-flash-crash-reignites-circuit-breaker-debate?ea9c8a2de0ee111045601ab04d673622.

Baumeister, Dayna. *Biomimicry Resource Handbook: A Seed Bank of Best Practices.* Missoula, MT: Biomimicry 3.8, 2013.

Benyus, Janine. *Biomimicry: Innovation Inspired by Nature.* New York: William Morrow, 1997.

Berg, Ann. "Commodity Funds in Retreat?" Special feature in *FAO Food Outlook*, June 2013: 66-68.

REFERENCES

Bernanke, Ben S. "Global Economic Integration: What's New and What's Not?" Speech at the Federal Reserve Bank of Kansas City's Thirtieth Annual Economic Symposium, Jackson Hole, Wyoming, August 25, 2006.

Bernanke, Ben S. "Community Development Financial Institutions: Challenges and Opportunities." Speech at the Global Financial Literacy Summit, Washington, D.C., June 17, 2009.

Block, Melissa. "2000 Commodities Act Paved Way for Problems." Interview with Michael Hirsch, *All Things Considered,* March 20, 2009. Link: http://www.npr.org/templates/story/story.php?storyId=102185942.

Buffett, Warren. "Letter to Shareholders." Berkshire Hathaway Annual Report, 2005. http://www.berkshirehathaway.com/2005ar/2005ar.pdf.

Cater, D.B., and N.R. Lawrie. "Some Histochemical and Biochemical Observations on the Preen Gland." *The Journal of Physiology* III, (1949): 231–243.

Charlson, Josh, with others. "Target-Date Series Research Paper: 2013 Survey." http://corporate.morningstar.com/us/documents/ResearchPapers/2013TargetDate.pdf.

Chase, Robin. SXSW Eco Keynote Address, October 2013. http://sxsw.com/music-film-interactive-sxsw-eco/news/2013/watch-sxsw-eco-2013-robin-chase-keynote

Christian, Leslie. "A New Foundation for Portfolio Management." *RSF Social Finance and Portfolio* 21, 2011. http://rsfsocialfinance.org/wp-content/uploads/downloads/2011/10/A-New-Foundation-for-Portfolio-Management.pdf.

"Credit Union Earnings Hit All-Time High", March 1, 2013. http://www.ncua.gov/News/Pages/NW20130301CUEarnings.aspx

Del Guercio, Diana, and Paula Tkac. "Star Power: The Effect of Morningstar Ratings on Mutual Fund Flows." November 2003. http://wwwdocs.fce.unsw.edu.au/banking/seminar/2004/Diane%20Del%20Guercio.pdf.

DeShutter, Oliver. "Food Commodities Speculation and Food Price Crises." *UN Special Rapporteur on the Right to Food*, September 2010.

Edelman. "Trust Barometer." 2013. http://www.edelman.com/insights/intellectual-property/trust-2013/trust-across-sectors/trust-in-financial-services.

Eichengreen, Barry. "Currency War or International Policy Coordination?" January 2013. http://emlab.berkeley.edu/~eichengr/curr_war_JPM_2013.pdf

Eichengreen, Barry. "Managing a Multiple Reserve Currency World." April 2010. http://emlab.berkeley.edu/~eichengr/managing_multiple_res_curr_world.pdf

Fernandes, Daniel, John Lynch, and Richard Netemeyer. "Financial Education and Downstream Financial Behaviors." Forthcoming in *Management Science,* October 8, 2013. See also: http://www.nytimes.com/2013/10/06/business/financial-literacy-beyond-the-classroom.html?pagewanted=all&_r=0.

Food and Agriculture Organization (FAO). "Food Outlook: Biannual Report on Global Food Markets." June 2013.

Fox, Justin. "The Economics of Well-Being." *Harvard Business Review,* January–February 2012. http://hbr.org/2012/01/the-economics-of-well-being/ar/.

Fullerton, John. "Commodities Are Different." Capital Institute post, August 5, 2013. http://capitalinstitute.org/blog/#.UtrbSNEo7IU http://capitalinstitute.org/blog/commodities-are-different-"full-world"-part-3 - .UjNYDaXIhwY.

General Electric company website. "Investor Relations section." http://www.ge.com/investor-relations.

Good Will Hunting, 1997. Gus Van Sant, director.

Gorzelak, P, Stolarski, J, Dubois, P, Kopp, C, Meibom, A. "26Mg Labeling of the Sea Urchin Regenerating Spine: Insights into Echinoderm Biomineralization Process." *Journal of Structural Biology*, 176 (2011): 119-126. via AskNature.org.

Gorelik, Richard B. "Presentation to the Commodity Futures Trading Commission Technology Advisory Committee." RGM Advisors, LLC. July 14, 2010. Retrieved from: http://www.capitolconnection.net/capcon/cftc/071410/Richard%20Gorelick%20Presentation%20to%20the%20CFTC%20Tech%20Committee.pdf.

Gosliner, Terry. "Nudibranchs, Corals, and Readers' Questions." *New York Times*, Scientist at Work. August 10, 2010. http://scientistatwork.blogs.nytimes.com/2010/08/10/nudibranchs-corals-and-readers-questions.

Grantham, Jeremy. "My Sister's Pension Assets and Agency Problems," April 2012. Published on gmo.com.

"The Financial Crisis Inquiry Report: Final Report of the National Commission on the Causes of the Financial and Economic Crisis in the United States." Official Report. Washington, D.C.: U.S. Government Printing Office. January, 2011.

Hafiz, and Daniel Ladinsky. *I Heard God Laughing: Poems of Hope and Joy*. New York: Penguin Books, 2006.

Hansch, Erick. "Research for the International Independence Institute, 1972." Notes via the Schumacher Library, via the New Economics Institute. http://neweconomy.net/publications/initial-results-wir-research-switzerland.

Harper, H.A., V.W. Rodwell, and P.A. Mayes. *Review of Physiological Chemistry*, 16th ed. Los Altos, California: Lange Medical Publications, 1977. Via howthingswork.com

Henderson, Hazel, and Janine Benyus. "Statement on Transforming Finance Based on Ethics and Life's Principles." 2012. http://www.ethicalmarkets.com/statement-on-transforming-finance-based-on-ethics-and-lifes-principles.

Holland, Jennifer S. "Living Color." *National Geographic*, June 2008. http://ngm.nationalgeographic.com/2008/06/nudibranchs/holland-text.

Investment Company Institute. "2013 Investment Company Fact Book," 53rd edition.

It's a Wonderful Life, 1946. Frank Capra, director.

Jones, Charles M. "What Do We Know About High-Frequency Trading?" *Columbia Business School Research Paper No. 13-11* (March 20, 2013). Available at SSRN: http://ssrn.com/abstract=2236201 or http://dx.doi.org/10.2139/ssrn.2236201.

Kaufman, Frederick. "The Food Bubble: How Wall Street Starved Millions and Got Away with It." *Harper's Magazine*, June 2010, 27-34.

Keller, Laurent, and Elizabeth Gordon. *The Lives of Ants*. New York: Oxford University Press, 2009.

Kennedy, Robert F. Remarks at the University of Kansas, March 18, 1968. Transcript from the John F. Kennedy Presidential Library and Museum. See: http://www.jfklibrary.org/Research/Research-Aids/Ready-Reference/RFK-Speeches/Remarks-of-Robert-F-Kennedy-at-the-University-of-Kansas-March-18-1968.aspx

Kier, William M., and Andrew M. Smith. "The Structure and Adhesive Mechanism of Octopus Suckers." *Integrative and Comparative Biology 42(6)* (2002):1146–1153. http://dx.doi.org/10.1093/icb/42.6.1146.

Knight, Frank H. *Risk, Uncertainty, and Profit*. Boston: Houghton and Mifflin, 1921. http://www.econlib.org/library/Knight/knRUP.html. Chapter 1, I.I.26.

Krugman, Paul. "The International Role of the Dollar: Theory and Prospect." *National Bureau of Economic Research*, 1984: Exchange Rate Theory and Practice, 263-264. http://nber.org/chapters/c6838.pdf. Krugman's description in turn is largely based on the work of B.J. Cohen, *The Future of Sterling as an International Currency*. London: Macmillan, 1971.

Lagi, M., K.Z. Bertrand, and Y. Bar-Yam. "Food Crises: A Quantitative Model of Food Prices Including Speculators and Ethanol." http://necsi.edu/research/social/food_prices.pdf.

Lagi, M., K.Z. Bertrand, and Y. Bar-Yam. "The Food Crises and Political Instability in North Africa and the Middle East." *New England Complex Systems Institute*, arXiv:1108.2455. August 10, 2011. http://necsi.edu/research/social/food_crises.pdf.

Liechti, Felix, and others. "First Evidence of a 200-Day Nonstop Flight in a Bird." *Nature Communications* 4, article 2554, October 8, 2013. Cited by *Smithsonian Magazine*, http://blogs.smithsonianmag.com/science/2013/10/this-bird-can-stay-in-flight-for-six-months-straight/?utm_source=smithsoniantopic&utm_medium=email&utm_campaign=20131013-Weekender.

Loutskina, Elena. "The Role of Securitization in Bank Liquidity and Funding Management," draft, 2010.

Lynch, Peter. *Beating the Street.* New York: Simon and Schuster, 1993.

Madrigal, Alexis C. "No Easy Tech Explanation for What Caused Wall St. 'Flash Crash.'" *The Atlantic,* July, 14, 2010, http://www.theatlantic.com/technology/archive/2010/07/no-easy-tech-explanation-for-what-caused-wall-st-flash-crash/59766.

Mauboussin, Michael J., with Tim Sullivan. "Embracing Complexity", interview in *Harvard Business Review,* September 2011.

Mauboussin, Michael J. "Interdisciplinary Perspectives on Risk." *Mauboussin on Strategy,* Legg Mason Capital Management, August 15, 2006.

Mauboussin, Michael J. *Think Twice.* Boston: Harvard Business Press, 2009.

McFarland, D. *A Dictionary of Animal Behaviour.* New York: Oxford Press, 2006.

Mills, L. Scott, and others. "Camouflage Mismatch in Seasonal Coat Color Due to Decreased Snow Duration." *Proceedings of the National Academy of Sciences of the United States of America,* Vol. 110 no. 18. http://www.pnas.org/content/110/18/7360.

Morrison, Wayne M. and Marc Labonte. "China's Holdings of U.S. Securities: Implications for the U.S. Economy." *Congressional Research Service,* August 19, 2013. http://www.fas.org/sgp/crs/row/RL34314.pdf.

Nakamoto, Satoshi. "Bitcoin: A Peer-to-Peer Electronic Cash System." October 31, 2008. http://bitcoin.org/bitcoin.pdf.

The New York Times. "Declining US High Frequency Trading." October 15, 2012. Data source: TABB Group. http://www.nytimes.com/interactive/2012/10/15/business/Declining-US-High-Frequency-Trading.html?ref=business.

Nørgaard, Thomas and Marie Dacke. "Fog-Basking Behaviour and Water Collection Efficiency in Namib Desert Darkling Beetles." *Frontiers in Zoology* 2010 7:23; also M.K. Seely, C.J. Lewis, K.A. O'Brien, and A.E. Suttle. "Fog Response of Tenebrionid Beetles in the Namib Desert." *Journal of Arid Environments* 6(2) (1983): 135–143. Via AskNature.org.

Pennsylvania State University. "Mammoth Genome Project." http://mammoth.psu.edu/howCloseElephantMammoth.html.

Phillips, Christopher, with Francis Kinniry Jr. and Todd Schlanger. "The Case for Index-Fund Investing." Vanguard, April 2013. Fund performance data from Morningstar. https://personal.vanguard.com/pdf/s296.pdf.

Phillips, Don, and Paul Kaplan (work at Morningstar). "The Morningstar Approach to Mutual Fund Analysis—Part II": 177–178.

Pinsky, Mark. "The CDFI Data Project: Fiscal Year 2008," Eighth Edition.

Pickrell, John. "Peacock Plumage Secrets Uncovered." *National Geographic News*, October 17, 2003.

Plato, Henry Cary, George Burges, and Henry Davis. *The Works of Plato*, Volume 6. London: George Bell and Sons, 1902.

Pollan, Michael. *The Omnivore's Dilemma: A Natural History of Four Meals*. New York: Penguin Books, 2007.

Pollan, Michael. "What's Eating America?" *Smithsonian*, June 15, 2006.

"The Price of Protest, So Far." Graphic from *The Economist*, July 14, 2011. http://www.economist.com/blogs/dailychart/2011/07/arab-spring-death-toll.

PriceMetrix. "The State of Retail Wealth Management: Third Annual Report." February 2013. http://www.pricemetrix.com/cms/wp-content/uploads/PriceMetrix-Insights_The-State-of-Retail-Wealth-Management-2012_English.pdf.

Richards, Vincent. *The Landmarks of Snake Poison Literature*. Calcutta: Thacker, Spink and Co., 1886. https://play.google.com/store/books/details?id=aeoyAQAAMAAJ&rdid=book-aeoyAQAAMAAJ&rdot=1.

Roach, John. "No Nemo: Anemones, Not Parents, Protect Clownfish." *National Geographic News* (2003) [Internet], Accessed August 27, 2007. AskNature.org. Also J.T. Szczebak, R.P. Henry, F.A. Al-Horani, and N.E. Chadwick. "Anemonefish Oxygenate Their Anemone Hosts at Night." *The Journal of Experimental Biology* 216 (2013): 970-976.

Robertson, David, and Bill Breen. *Brick by Brick: How LEGO Rewrote the Rules of Innovation and Conquered the Global Toy Industry*. New York: Random House, 2013.

Robertson, Paul Kemp. TED Talk on Bitcoin. http://www.ted.com/talks/paul_kemp_robertson_bitcoin_sweat_tide_meet_the_future_of_branded_currency.html?source=facebook#.UfZqbzVjjSt.facebook.

Sargut, Gokce, and Rita Gunther McGrath. "Learning to Live with Complexity." *Harvard Business Review,* September 1, 2011.

Scheffel A., N. Poulsen, S. Shian, and N. Kroger. "Nanopatterned Protein Microrings from a Diatom That Direct Silica Morphogenesis." *PNAS* 108(8) (2011): 3175–3180. http://www.asknature.org/.

Schmitt, Rick. "Prophet and Loss." *Stanford Magazine*, March/April 2009. http://alumni.stanford.edu/get/page/magazine/article/?article_id=30885.

Schroeder, Alice. *The Snowball: Warren Buffett and the Business of Life*. New York: Bantam Dell, 2008.

Schumacher Center for a New Economics: http://centerforneweconomics.org/content/active-local-currencies.

Seeley, Thomas D. *Honeybee Democracy*. Princeton, NJ: Princeton University Press, 2010.

Sharma, Shefali, and Steve Suppan. "Commodity Market Deregulation and Food Prices." Institute for Agriculture and Trade Policy Presentation at UNCATD Symposium, June 22, 2011. http://www.iatp.org/files/Commodity market deregulation and food prices.pdf.

Slow Money website. http://slowmoney.org.

Sorkin, Andrew Ross. "Doubts Raised on Value of Investment Consultants to Pensions." *The New York Times*, September 30, 2013.

Steinbeck, John. *East of Eden*. New York: Penguin Books, 1952.

Stodder, James. "Complementary Credit Networks and Macro-Economic Stability: Switzerland's Wirtschaftsring." *Journal of Economic Behavior & Organization*, 72 (October, 2009): 79–95. http://ewp.rpi.edu/hartford/~stoddj/BE/WIR_Update.pdf.

Swack, Michael, Jack Northrup, and Eric Hangen. "CDFI Industry Analysis Summary Report." *Carsey Institute*, Spring 2012.

Switek, Brian. "In Evolution's Race, Horseshoe Crabs Took a Slower Pace." *Wired*, November 22, 2011. With reference to: Feldmann, R.,

Schweitzer, C., Dattilo, B., & Farlow, J. (2011). "Remarkable Preservation of a New Genus and Species of Limuline Horseshoe Crab From the Cretaceous of Texas, USA." *Palaeontology, 54* (6), 1337-1346 DOI: 10.1111/j.1475-4983.2011.01103.x.

Tattersall, G.J., D.V. Andrade, and A.S. Abe. "Heat Exchange from the Toucan Bill Reveals a Controllable Vascular Thermal Radiator." *Science* 325(5939) (2009): 468–470. Referenced by: http://www.asknature.org/strategy/1efca39a0abb5ecd20edc6a4fdef8a2a.

Thompson Reuters. "Debt Capital Markets Review: Managing Underwriters." First Quarter 2013.

Thornton, A., and K. McAuliffe. *Science* 313 (5784) (July 14, 2006): 227–229.

The Economist. "Toxic Medicine," January 5, 2013. http://www.economist.com/news/science-and-technology/21569015-snake-venom-being-used-cure-rather-kill-toxic-medicine.

Tree of Life website: tolweb.org/Diatoms/21810.

Tricarico, Elena, and Francesca Gherardi. "Resource Assessment in Hermit Crabs: The Worth of Their Own Shell." *Behavioral Ecology* 18 (3) (2007): 615–620.

United States CFTC and SEC. "Findings Regarding the Market Events of May 6, 2010: Report of the Staffs of the CFTC and SEC to the Join Advisory Committee on Emerging Regulatory Issues." September 30, 2010. http://www.sec.gov/news/studies/2010/marketevents-report.pdf.

Welch, Jack. "Eating and Dreaming." Post for *Linked In*, July 25, 2013. http://www.linkedin.com/today/post/article/20130725154204-86541065-eating-and-dreaming.

Young, Iris Marion. "Responsibility and Global Labor Justice." *Journal of Political Philosophy* 12 (4) (2004): 365–388.

Zelizer, Viviana. *American Behavioral Scientist* (2007): 1061, referencing her earlier work, *The Social Meaning of Money.*

Acknowledgments

Like any good ecosystem, this book has a number of vibrant, intersecting webs and layers of community that have contributed to its creation. Some of these ecosystem species are highly visible and their functions are direct and tangible; others are less apparent and their support is indirect, but just as vital, and just as appreciated.

Most directly, I want to thank Janine Benyus and Hazel Henderson, dear mentors and co-creators of Ethical Biomimicry Finance. Both of these women have intellectual rigor, clarity of vision, and warmth of spirit—a rare trifecta of gifts. Their work has formed the rich soil that roots and nourishes the ideas in this book, and their personal support has nourished me throughout the research and writing process.

Along with Janine and Hazel is a growing community of thinkers and do-ers in biomimimicry and investing, including educators, scientists, business leaders, and more. I am lucky to include Dayna Baumeister, Chris Allen, Beth Rattner, Bryony Schwan, Nicole Hagerman Miller, Toby Herzlich, Erin Leitch, Sherry Ritter, Rosalinda Sanquiche,

Lina Constantinovici, Eva Willmann de Donlea, Stuart Williams, Stuart Valentine, and Susan Davis as colleagues, mentors, and friends. Additionally, I benefitted tremendously from cross-pollination with my colleagues in the 2013 Biomimicry Specialist cohort, especially Victoria Keziah and Ken McLellan (long live Team SuperOrg!).

In exploring biomimicry investing I have come to appreciate the power of adaptation more and more, and so I am increasingly grateful for the mentors, colleagues, and friends who have adapted along with me from my perch at Fidelity to my perch at Honeybee Capital. To all of my ecosystem connections who are engaged in investing and finance, especially the giant web of friends from Fidelity, I am deeply indebted. It is thanks to you that I know investing as a noble, valuable profession, not just a business.

Every ecosystem also needs sources of ongoing nourishment, and for me this has been found in people and organizations dedicated to creativity, curiosity, reflection, connection, and rigorous analysis. Thank you to Michael Mauboussin, Andrew Zolli and the PopTech group, the Harvard Divinity School community, the Ohana Investment Circle, and the complexity science networks of the Santa Fe Institute and the New England Complex Systems Institute. All of the authors of material in the Resources section have also provided ongoing insight and inspiration, some from afar and some from a-near. Raj Panjabi and the team at Last Mile Health, the Common Impact family, and everyone involved with Wellesley College and Habitat for Humanity have helped to re-center my work in service through their inspiring examples.

Stephanie Schacht deserves her own shining star on our ecosystem map, as she provided research support in every form – philosophical, creative, and analytical. My brother described Stephanie as the one person on earth with the breadth of knowledge and interests needed to simultaneously research questions like, "What is the best theory on money as an expression of social connection?" and "How much was total CDO issuance in 2Q 2006?" He was right.

One of the most important considerations for ecosystem health is the surrounding environment, the operating conditions that influence the system day in and day out. I am grateful to Jill Friedlander, Erika Heilman, Shevaun Betzler, Jill Schoenhaut, and the whole Bibliomotion team, for setting remarkably favorable operating conditions throughout this process. Barbara Henricks, Margaret Kingsbury, Rusty Shelton, and their colleagues at Cave Henricks Shelton, terrific navigators of the media web, have ensured that this message is heard. Jurriaan Kamp and Helene De Puy saved the day when we were stumped with title discussions. The fantastic team at Guts & Glory has helped to align belief and practice and visual image for Honeybee Capital in a way that I never imagined possible. Thank you, thank you, thank you.

Dearest to me, I am thankful for my own little subspecies within the ecosystem, my family. When I was seven years old and told my parents I was going to be President of the United States, they did not laugh; that's pretty much all you need to know about our supportive family environment. My Wellesley sisters—all of them—and my Newton friends have provided inspiration and connection and comfort over long stretches of time and space, cushioning some disruptions and gently encouraging others, just exactly as needed.

Finally, I am grateful for my literal ecosystem, my corner of Massachusetts full of sugar maples and swampy bogs and bluebirds and rolling hills and honeybees and a big brown thing that lives under the porch. I can't wait to see what wisdom they will share with me in the time to come.

Index

A
abstraction of activity, 62–63
abundance, 161
Acumen, 131
adaptability, 14, 117–136, 160–161
 assessment tools and, 117–122
 creativity and, 131
 diversity and, 118, 120, 122
 evolution of, 131–133
 evolving to survive and, 144
 mutual funds and, 125–131
 pathway to practice of, 133–135
 reactivity in, 126
 resilience and, 118, 119–120, 121–122
 self-renewal and integrity in, 118, 119, 121, 126
 sowing seeds of, 135–136
 style box tool and, 126–129
 translating to investing, 123–124
 variation and, 129–130
agency, 22
Airbnb, 152
alignment, 19–20
Allen, Chris, 18

B
bank consolidations, 65–66
banking, 65–66, 147, 149
barter, 145–146, 151–152
Baumeister, Dayna, 17, 18
B-corp (benefit corporation) movement, 91
Benyus, Janine, 9, 17, 18, 54
biomimicry framework, 9–11
 ancient wisdom in, 17
 context in, 19
 efficiency vs. effectiveness and, 27–47
 evolving to survive, 136–151
 getting started with, 22–24
 locally attuned, 95–116
 mindfulness in, 117–136
 multilayered approach in, 20
 philosophy and practice in, 16
 practice in, 19–24
 roots of, 13–18
 scaling with, 20
 what it is not, 21
Biomimicry Specialist education program, 17–18
Bitcoin, 147, 151, 152
blame, 17

bottom-up activity, 73, 74, 75–77, 83–84, 87
"Break Up with Your Mega-Bank," 65
Buffett, Warren, 38, 121
Business Alliance for Local Living Economies (BALLE), 113–114
Buzzcar, 152

C
Calvert Foundation, 45
Capital Institute, 111
Chase, Robin, 152
Cheez Whiz, 50, 67
Chicago Board of Trade, 108
choice, power of, 165–167
closed systems, 142–143, 154
collateralized debt obligation (CDO), 60–64
collateralized mortgage obligation (CMO), 60–64
comfort, 10
command-and-control management, 77
commercial traders, 105
Commodities Futures Trading Commission (CTFC), 85–86
commodities markets, 104–112, 146
Commodity Futures Modernization Act, 108
Commodity Futures Trading Commission (CFTC), 108
community. *See also* connections
  commodities markets and, 104–112
  in finance, 58–59
  local, attunement with, 95–101
  mortgage-backed securities and, 60
community agriculture programs, 132–133
community development financial institutions (CDFIs), 114
complexity
  complication vs., 42–43
  in mortgage-backed securities, 60–64
  regulatory, 76–77
compliance agreements, 76–77
complication
  complexity vs., 42–43
  cost of for investors, 38–42
  as duplication, 45
  efficiency and, 47
  simplicity vs., 49–69
  through investment helpers, 36–43
  unnecessary, 27–28
connections, 95–116, 159–160
  in consumer banking, 65–66
  cooperation and, 97, 98, 100–101
  eroded by tools, 4–6
  growth and, 79
  for simplicity vs. synthetic investing, 57–59
context, 19, 23–24
  for effective investing, 34–35
  growth and, 79
  local community and, 97, 100, 115–116
cooperation, 97, 98, 100–101, 116
  commodities markets and, 106, 112
corn, food commodity markets and, 110–111
creativity, 3–4, 20
  adaptability and, 131
  evolving to survive and, 153–154
  limits as spur to, 55–56
credit unions, 65
crowd funding, 66
curiosity, 21
currencies, evolution of, 145–151, 145–153, 155
cyclic processes, 97, 99, 106, 112

INDEX

D
data gathering, 6, 135–136
  open inquiry in, 21
  reshuffling information and, 139, 140, 148, 150
Davis, Susan, 132
decentralization, 118, 119–120, 121–122, 136
decision making, 6–9, 11, 162. *See also* investment tools
"Declaration of Interdependence," 91
decomposition into benign constituents, 51, 53–54, 61
derivatives, commodities markets, 108
development. *See* growth
diatoms, 52–53
diversity, 118, 120, 122, 136
  in mutual funds, 126, 129
duplication, 45
durability. *See* resilience
"duration trading" approaches, 136

E
East of Eden (Steinbeck), 165
economic theory, 15–16
Edelman Trust Barometer, 147
effectiveness, 27–47
  in investing, 33–47
  of mutual funds, 126, 129
  pathway to, 45–46
  purpose and, 36–43
  relationship with efficiency, 31–32
efficiency, 27–47
  connections vs., 4–6
  in investing, 33–47
  of mutual funds, 126, 129
  pathway to practice of, 45–46
  purpose in, 36–43
  relationship with effectiveness, 31–32
  resource, 28–32, 46–47
  systemic, 46
  time frame and, 32
  tools in, 4–6
  uncertainty and, 133–134
electronic currencies, 147, 151–153
embodiment, 141
energy efficiency, 28–32
engagement, 3–4
equity investing, 65
ethanol policy, 109–111
evolving to survive, 137–155
  currency, 145–153, 150
  definition of success and, 141–142, 144–145
  embodiment of, 141
  integrating the unexpected and, 139, 140, 150
  open vs. closed systems and, 142–143
  pathway to practice in, 153–154
  replicating what works and, 139–140, 150
  reshuffling information and, 139, 140, 150
  sowing seeds of, 154–155
  translating to investing, 144–145
exchange, 13, 145–151
exploration, 96–97
extension of activity, 62–63

F
failure
  fast, 88
  rates of, 141
farmer's markets, 132–133
fear, 142
feedback loops
  in commodities markets, 106–107
  commodity markets and, 112
  crucial components of, 99–100
  in early-stage ventures, 88
  in high-frequency trading, 87

feedback loops (*cont.*)
locally attuned, 97, 99–100, 101, 116
in quarterly earnings releases, 102–104
resilience and, 135–136
style box tool and, 128
Fidelity Magellan Fund, 141–142
finance, 13–15
financial markets
2008 financial crisis and, 62–63
changes in, 3–6
commodities, 106–112
flash crashes, 81, 84–86
reframing, 22–23
financial system
fissures in current, 159–161
resilience of, 15
"first loss" investments, 131
flash crashes, 81, 84–86
flexibility, 10, 14, 160–161
food commodities, 107–114
Freecycle, 152
Fullerton, John, 111
"full-spectrum" investing, 131–132
function
of currency, 147–148
of effective investing, 45–47
fitting form to, 29, 30–31, 47
of investing, 34–35
in mutual funds, 38
of mutual funds, 125–131
need-based, 30–31, 35–36
overloading, 155
overshadowed by finance, 13–15
simplicity and, 57–58
of ultra-helped investment, 42
fund of funds products, 39

G
General Electric, 103
globalization, 97, 104–112
gold standard, 145
Good Will Hunting, 34
Gramm, Leach, Bliley Act, 108
Grantham, Jeremy, 142
Grantham Mayo van Otterloo, 142
Green America, 65
growth
of beehives, 78
bottom-up, 73, 74, 75–77, 83–84, 87
changing definitions of, 89–90
in early-stage ventures, 88–91
evolution of, 88–91
high-frequency trading and, 81–87
integrated point of view for, 75
integrating with development, 71–94
modular/nested components and, 73, 83, 87
multidimensional, 89–91
optimization vs. maximization of, 71–94
pathway to practice for, 92–93
purpose of, 80
self-organized, 73, 74–75, 84, 87
sowing seeds of integrated, 93–94
translating to investing, 78–81

H
Habitat for Humanity, 95–96, 115
heat maps, 4–5
hedge funds, 39
costs of, 40–41
Henderson, Hazel, 9, 17, 18
high-frequency trading, 81–87, 92
Honeybee Capital, 9
honeybees
adaptability of, 123
decision making by, 6–8
evolution of to survive, 143
integrated growth and development by, 78

- life-friendly chemistry by, 54
- locally attuned, 102
- resource and energy efficiency of, 33

I

impact investing, 44–45, 132–133
index funds, 36–37, 39
information
- locally attuned, 97, 99–100
- sharing for collective decision making, 6–7

inspiration, 10
integrated approaches, 10
- for growth and development, 71–94

integrating the unexpected, 139, 140, 148, 150
integrity, 118, 119
intentions, 153
intervention, currency as, 149
investing
- by actual investors, 66
- adaptability in, 123–136
- alignment of with nature, 13
- biomimicry-based framework for, 9–11, 13–18
- decision making for, 6–9
- efficiency vs. effectiveness in, 33–47
- as embodied belief, 165–166
- fissures in current system of, 159–161
- function vs. finance in, 13–15
- growth and optimization of, 71–94
- high-frequency trading, 81–87
- impact, 44–45
- life-friendly, 56–59
- locally attuned, 102–114
- need-based, 35–36, 44–45
- as profession, 15–18
- purpose in, 36–43
- rearranging with nature, 22
- reframing, 22–23
- risk management in, 14, 15
- synthetic vs. simple, 49–69
- transactional vs. relational, 115
- ultra-helped, 40–42

investment advisors, 39
investment tools, 11, 117–136
- complication through, 36–43
- connections eroded by, 4–6
- as drivers of investing, 14
- heat maps, 4–5
- mutual fund, 125–131
- reorienting toward resilience, 134–135
- risk management and, 124, 129–131
- style box, 127–128

invoicing, 149
It's a Wonderful Life, 59–60

K

Kant, Immanuel, 13
Kennedy, Robert, 89–90
Kickstarter, 66
Kiva, 66
Knight, Frank, 130

L

leadership, 76–77
LIBOR, 111
life-friendly chemistry, 51–54
- decomposition into benign constituents, 51, 53–54, 64
- do chemistry in water, 52–53, 63
- limits and, 54–56
- mortgage-backed securities and, 59–64
- selective building with a small subset of elements, 51, 53, 63

limitations, 54–56, 131

local attunement and responsiveness. *See also* community
- commodities markets and, 104–112
- cooperative relationships and, 97, 98, 100–101, 106, 112, 116
- as dynamic, responsive process, 101
- evolution of, 112–114
- evolving to survive and, 144
- feedback loops/information flows and, 97, 99–100, 112, 116
- of honeybees, 102
- leveraging cyclic processes and, 97, 99, 106, 112
- pathway to practice of, 114–115
- readily available materials/energy and, 97–98, 106, 111
- sowing seeds of, 115–116
- translating to investing, 102–104

long-term approach, 137–155
- definitions of success and, 141–142
- evolving to survive, 137–143

Lynch Peter, 141–142

M

management, 76–77

Mauboussin, Michael, 130

maximization, optimization vs. *See* optimization

mentors, 88–89

modular/nested components, 73, 83, 87, 88

Morningstar, 127–128

mortgage-backed securities, 59–64

Mosaic Energy, 66

multidimensional perspectives, 89–91, 121–122

multifunctional design, 28
- evolving to survive and, 150–151
- of mutual funds, 37
- of ultra-helped investment, 41

multilayered approaches, 20

Munger, Charlie, 121

mutual funds, 36–38
- analytics for, 125–131
- costs of, 39
- "go-anywhere," 125–126
- style box tool for, 127–129
- "target date," 128

N

nature, as model, mentor, measure, and muse, 20

need
- in investing, 34–35
- reconnecting investment with, 44–45
- simplicity and, 66–67

New England Complex Systems Institute (NECSI), 109–110

New York Stock Exchange, 85

nonjudgmental systems, 10

nontoxic production, 50–56
- mortgage-backed securities and, 60–64
- sowing seeds of, 68–69
- translating to investing, 56–59

O

openmindedness, 23–24

open systems, 142–143, 154

optimism, 161–162

optimization, 19, 71–94
- bottom-up, 73, 74, 75–77, 83–84, 87
- integrated point of view for, 75
- integrating growth and development for, 71–77
- modular/nested components and, 73, 83, 87
- pathway to practice for, 92–93
- self-organization and, 73, 74–75, 84, 87
- translating to investing, 78–81

P
participation, 17
patience, 23–24
peer collaboration, 152
peer-to-peer lending, 44
perspectives, 160
 multidimensional, 89–91, 121–122
 romanticized, 10, 21
planning, 76–77
Plato, 165
Pollan, Michael, 110
pollination, 143, 155
portfolio theory, 124, 134–135
Principles of Ethical Biomimicry Finance (Henderson, Benyus, Sanquiche), 18
proactivity, 3–4
processes
 life-friendly chemistry and, 51–54
 low-energy, 28, 37, 41
 of mutual funds, 37
 in ultra-helped investment, 41
prosperity, definitions of, 89–90
purpose
 appropriate, 135–136
 complicated vs. complex, 42–43
 in effective and efficient investing, 36–43
 efficiency and, 45–46
 growth and, 80, 92, 93
 in nontoxic investing, 68–69

Q
quarterly earnings releases, 102–104
quietness, 23–24
Quotron, 4–5

R
rearranging, 22
recycling, 29, 30
 in mutual funds, 38
 in ultra-helped investment, 41–42
redundancy, 118, 119–120, 121–122, 136
refocusing, 133
refraining, 23–24
reframing, 22–23
regenerative systems, 160
regulatory systems, 76–77
 food commodity markets, 108, 109–111, 113
relational investing, 115
replicating what works, 139–140, 148, 150
resilience, 10, 14, 160–161
 adaptation and, 118, 119–120, 121–122, 123–124
 evolving to survive, 137–155
 of financial system, 15
 multidimensional growth and, 90–91
 multidimensionality of, 121–122
 of mutual funds, 126, 129
 reorientation toward, 133–135
 sowing seeds of, 135–136
resource efficiency, 28–32
 form and function in, 29, 30–31
 in investing, 33–36
 low-energy processes and, 29–30
 of mutual funds, 37–38
 recycling and, 29, 30
 sowing seeds of in investing, 46–47
 time frame and, 32
responsibility, 17
Rilke, Rainer Maria, 163
risk and risk management, 14
 adaptability vs., 124
 fear and, 142
 focus on, 15
 by measuring it, 129–131
 portfolio theory on, 134–135
 resilience and, 135–136
 uncertainty vs., 129–130, 133–134

romanticized perspectives, 10, 21
RSF Social Finance, 45

S
Sanquiche, Rosalinda, 18
scalability, 79
scale, 20
Securities Exchange Commission (SEC), 85–86, 87
Seeley, Tom, 6–8
self-organization, 73, 74–75, 84, 87
self-renewal, 118, 119, 121
  in mutual funds, 126, 128–129
self-sustaining activity, 19–20
simplicity
  bottom-up activity and, 76–77
  elegance of, 54, 68–69
  evolution of in investing, 65–66
  life-friendly chemistry and, 51–54
  limits and, 54–56
  mortgage-backed securities and, 59–64
  nontoxic production and, 50–56
  pathway to practice in, 66–68
  sowing seeds of, 68–69
  synthetic vs., 49–69
Slow Money movement, 113
SoCap conference, 132
Social Progress Index, 89
social unrest, food commodity markets and, 110–111
speculation, 14, 107–113
"spin class" approach to trading, 82, 92, 93–94
Stamp, Josiah Charles, 159
standardization, 122, 128
Steinbeck, John, 165
stewardship, 17
stockpicking, 39
style box tool, 127–128
success, definitions of, 141–142, 144–145, 153–154, 155
supply and demand, 109–110
sustainability, 9, 19
synthetic securities, 49–56, 56–57, 58–59. *See also* simplicity

T
TaskRabbit, 152
technology, 4–6, 152–153
thinking, 3–4, 11, 165–167
time frames
  efficiency and, 32
  long-term, 137–151
timshel, 165–167
tools. *See* investment tools
toxic securities, 50
transactional investing, 115
Transition Movement, 132
transparency, 153
TriLinc Global, 45
trust, 146–147, 153
tulip mania, 35
Twinkie portfolios, 66–68

U
uncertainty, 129–130, 133–134. *See also* risk and risk management

V
value, storage of, 148–149
value systems, 7, 165–166
variation, 118, 119–120, 121–122, 129–130, 136

W
waggle dance, 102
Welch, Jack, 32, 103
White Dog Café, 90–91
Wicks, Judy, 90–91
WIR, 151–152

Z
Zipcar, 152

About the Author

Katherine Collins is Founder and CEO of Honeybee Capital, a research firm focused on pollinating ideas that reconnect investing with the real world. After a long and successful career as head of research and portfolio manager at Fidelity Management & Research Company, Katherine set out to re-integrate her investment philosophy with the broader world, traveling as a pilgrim and volunteer, earning her MTS degree at Harvard Divinity School, and studying biomimicry and the natural world as guides for investing in an integrated, regenerative way, in service to our communities and our planet. She lives in Massachusetts with several thousand honeybees.

More details about Katherine, The Nature of Investing, and Honeybee Capital can be found at honeybeecapital.com.